DEVELOPING COGNITIVE-BEHAVIOURAL COUNSELLING

Developing Counselling, edited by Windy Dryden, is an innovative series of books which provides counsellors and counselling trainees with practical hints and guidelines on the problems they face in the counselling process. The books assume that readers have a working knowledge of the approach in question and, in a clear and accessible fashion, show how the counsellor can more effectively translate that knowledge into everyday practice.

Books in the series include:

Developing the Practice of Counselling
Windy Dryden and Colin Feltham

Developing Counsellor Supervision
Colin Feltham and Windy Dryden

Developing Counsellor Training
Windy Dryden and Colin Feltham

Developing Person-Centred Counselling
Dave Mearns

Developing Psychodynamic Counselling
Brendan McLoughlin

Developing Rational Emotive Behavioural Counselling
Windy Dryden and Joseph Yankura

DEVELOPING COGNITIVE-BEHAVIOURAL COUNSELLING

Michael J. Scott,
Stephen G. Stradling
and Windy Dryden

SAGE Publications
London • Thousand Oaks • New Delhi

SAGE Publications Ltd
6 Bonhill Street
London EC2A 4PU

SAGE Publications Inc
2455 Teller Road
Thousand Oaks, California 91320

SAGE Publications India Pvt Ltd
32, M-Block Market
Greater Kailash – I
New Delhi 110 048

British Library Cataloguing in Publication data

A catalogue record for this book is available from the British Library.

ISBN 0 8039 7893 6
ISBN 0 8039 7894 4 (pbk)

Library of Congress catalog card number 95–074694

Typeset by Mayhew Typesetting, Rhayader, Powys
Printed in Great Britain by Biddles Ltd, Guildford

Contents

List of Tables and Figures

Tables

Figures

Introduction

Cognitive-behavioural counselling takes note of the everyday observation that people respond differently to the same situation. As early as the first century AD the Stoic Philosopher Epictetus wrote 'People are disturbed not so much by events as by the views which they take of them'. The explanation given by cognitive-behaviour theorists, such as Beck et al. (1979) and Ellis (1962), for this phenomenon is that an individual's interpretation of a situation has a major influence on his or her subsequent emotions and behaviour. For example, one person may feel upset and angry that a colleague, John, did not greet him or her in the corridor at work, interpreting it as a personal slight. Another person similarly 'ignored', may feel pity, saying 'John has real problems, he is so mixed up' and can more easily shrug off the encounter. That is, the situation can be viewed from different angles and some angles may be more adaptive than others.

The prime therapeutic tasks in the cognitive-behaviour therapies as originally developed by Beck et al. (1979) and Ellis (1962) are to help clients check out whether they are making the most adaptive and rational interpretation of a situation and engage in behaviours consistent with this 'new angle'. The metaphor underlying the cognitive-behavioural approach is one of an individual operating a camera with optional lenses, filters and settings. This model carries with it the implication that the person with a mental health problem is not qualitatively different from a person without a problem. Rather the former almost habitually has his or her 'camera' focused in such a way as to take unrealistic 'photographs' of situations. This approach helps lead to an equalising of the relationship between counsellor and client.

Cognitive-behaviour theory makes a distinction between cognitive products, cognitive processes and cognitive schemas. The self-talk of John's colleague in the scenario above, 'He has got real problems' is an example of a cognitive product. The products may be at the forefront of a person's consciousness or at the edge of awareness, that is they may take more or less exploration to discover in counselling. Cognitive products are not confined to covert verbalisations but may also include images and they share a reflex quality, often seeming to occur without conscious and deliberate effort, and for that reason they are often termed 'automatic thoughts'. The essence of the cognitive-behavioural approach is that cognitive products interface between situations and emotional, behavioural and physiological responses, and as such the approach is an important elaboration of the earlier stimulus–response model of human behaviour.

Cognitive processes operate at a less manifest level and represent the mechanisms by which individuals come to formulate the judgements, evaluations, expectations, perceptions and so on that dominate their awareness. A central theme in Beck et al.'s (1979) formulation of depression is that depressive symptoms are mediated by faulty thinking patterns. For example, depressed individuals may generalise from a single event to a wide range of events (overgeneralisation), exaggerate the negative impact of undesirable outcomes (magnification, catastrophising), or jump to conclusions in the absence of corroborative evidence (arbitrary inference). Cognitive schemas are the templates an individual uses to process information, they are thought to operate at a structural level to store, organise, integrate and direct the processing of personally relevant information. Schemas of self-referent information (self-schemas) are thought to play a central role in depression. According to Beck's formulation, negative self-schemas comprise a highly organised network of stored personal information – primarily unfavourable – along with rules for evaluating one's worth or value as a person. In depression these schemas become activated resulting in the tendency to view oneself unfavourably and to interpret one's life (past, current and future) in a predominantly negative fashion. In addition activated negative self-schemas facilitate the retrieval of information that support their validity. The distinctions between cognitive products, cognitive structures and cognitive schemas are somewhat arbitrary but have served to foster the development of cognitive-behavioural counselling (CBC) so far and indeed much of the further evolution of CBC is likely to be focused on the elaboration of cognitive schemas.

In CBC as developed by Beck and Ellis most of the emphasis has been on bringing about emotional and behavioural change by means of a change in cognitions, though it is acknowledged by these authors that the three reciprocally interact. The cognitive model is shown in Figure I.1

Inspection of Figure I.1 shows, for example, that it is perfectly consistent with the cognitive model to recommend a client to engage in exercise (a behaviour) as a way of reducing tension (physiology) which then relieves depressed mood (emotion) which may then lead to a less catastrophic appraisal (cognition) of

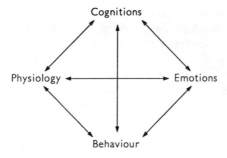

Figure I.1 *The cognitive model*

a current daily hassle. The counsellor can thus help the client by means of any of the four ports of entry, and whichever port is chosen will have ripple effects on other ports. Different psychological therapies have tended to emphasise particular ports as the target and one of the virtues of the cognitive model is that it legitimises diverse approaches and serves an integrative function.

Cognitive-behavioural counselling was developed as a brief form of individual treatment, programmes for disorders such as anxiety, depression and bulimia typically taking three to four months of weekly therapy sessions with occasional booster sessions in the year following. Because of its educative nature it has also lent itself to delivery in group format (Scott and Stradling, 1990).

The cognitive-behavioural approaches have certain commonalities which are now described in detail.

1   *Therapy begins with an elaborated well planned rationale.* This rationale provides the initial structure that helps the client to acquire the belief that it is possible to control his or her own behaviour. In practice this means explaining that in the ABC model it is the interpretation and evaluation of an event (B) that is the major influence on emotional response (C), rather than the event or stimulus (A) per se. Analogies are useful to convey this message. For example, 'The mind is like a camera, it depends on the settings and the lenses you chose as to what sort of photographs of events you take. It is possible to teach a person to choose the settings and lenses so that they receive more realistic pictures of the situation than the ones you are typically disturbed about.'

The rationale for the behavioural dimension of therapy is

usually explained in terms of activity as a prerequisite for a sense of mastery or pleasure. It is therefore necessary to overcome the inertia that emotional distress can produce.

The cognitive and behavioural dimensions overlap considerably. For example, a client may refuse to go to the theatre, something once enjoyed, resisting the behavioural task on the cognitive grounds that 'I know I am not going to enjoy it, so why bother'. This 'roadblock' would be tackled cognitively by suggesting that the thought that the play would not be enjoyed was a hypothesis, that the client does not have a crystal ball, and so needs to conduct an experiment to test the veracity of this prediction. At the start of therapy it is also important to outline the time scale of therapy, the likelihood of success and the importance of homework assignments.

2 *Therapy should provide training in skills that the client can utilise to feel more effective in handling daily life.* Clients are asked to record between sessions events that they experience as upsetting. These may be external events such as being criticised by a spouse, or internal events such as experiencing a sudden change of mood while looking out of the window watching the traffic go by. Having identified the triggering events (A) and the emotional responses (C) to these events, clients are asked to record what they might have said to themselves (B) to get so upset, that is, to find the Bs of their ABC model. Clients may have greater or less access to the Bs depending on whether they are at the forefront of their mind or at the edge of awareness. Part of the therapeutic skill lies in making the Bs explicit and then helping the client challenge whether or not they are valid and useful and by what authority they are held. For example a client who experiences a downturn in mood while watching the traffic may have been saying 'Life is just passing me by, I'm always getting myself into a bad mood, I'll always be this way, I'm a failure'. A more adaptive response might have been, 'I am only 40, life begins at 40, some things I have done well, some badly, its time I joined the human race!'.

3 *Therapy emphasises the independent use of skills by the client outside the therapy context.* If in the therapy session the therapist had, for example, drawn a client's attention to a constant theme of failure in the client's Bs, then there would be an expectation that outside therapy the client would immediately check out the failure theme when experiencing

emotional distress. First the client might be instructed to pause on noticing the first signs of emotional distress. Then the client should inspect likely self-talk triggers such as failure. Having identified which theme or themes are operative, the client would then apply the alternative rational response which had been selected and practised in therapy in order to behave in a way that could enhance a sense of mastery and pleasure.

4 *Therapy should encourage the client to attribute improvement in mood more to his or her own increased skilfulness rather than to the therapist's endeavours.* To the extent that a client sees an improvement in mood as a product of a change in thinking habits and behaviour the therapist will be able to terminate therapy. Clients can be prepared to make such attributions by the therapist's constant emphasis on the importance of homework assignments. Essentially the client is being taught a skill for independent use, and the more the skill is practised the more skilful the client will become.

Though cognitive-behavioural approaches have the commonalities set out above, they also have differences. Dobson (1988) has divided them into four broad categories: coping skills, problem solving, cognitive restructuring and structural cognitive therapy. Each of these are now briefly summarised.

1 *Coping skills*: Stress Inoculation Training (SIT; Meichenbaum, 1985) is the most well-known therapy in this category. SIT is aimed at the reduction and prevention of stress. Stress is viewed as an interaction between the individual and the environment. Both need to be targeted for change. At an individual level clients may be taught what to say to themselves and how to respond in situations that they find difficult.

2 *Problem solving*: Problem Solving Therapy (Nezu et al., 1989) has been the most widely applied therapy in this category. Problem solving is conceptualised as involving the following stages: problem orientation, i.e. 'locking on' to a problem; precise definition of the problem; the generation of as many alternative solutions as possible; choosing the best solution; planning implementation of the solution; and reviewing progress. If the chosen solution has not remedied the problem or only partially so, another solution is chosen, implemented and subsequently reviewed. This approach can be applied to both impersonal and interpersonal problems.

3   *Cognitive restructuring*: The two main therapies under this category are rational emotive therapy (RET; Ellis, 1962) and cognitive therapy (CT; Beck et al., 1979). RET contends that irrationality is a major cause of emotional disorder. Ellis (1962) has suggested that much of the neurotic person's thinking is dominated by 'musts', 'shoulds', 'oughts' and 'have tos'. From the inappropriate use of these moral imperatives, three tendencies may develop:

   (a) *'Awfulising'*, which is the tendency to overemphasise the negative aspect of an event.

   (b) *'I can't stand it-itis'*, which is the tendency to overemphasise the discomfort of a situation.

   (c) *'Damnation'*, which is the tendency to evaluate as 'Bad' the essence or human value of self and/or others as a result of the individual's behaviour.

   In CT it is maladaptive interpretations of situations that are viewed as exercising a pivotal role with regard to emotional distress rather than irrational beliefs. Beck et al. (1990) contend for example that an interpretation of a situation that was adaptive in childhood may become maladaptive in adulthood. For instance, an abused child may well conclude on the basis of experience that adults should be approached with great caution. This may lead to an unnecessary timidity with other people when themselves an adult.

   In CT clients are asked to collect data on their current maladaptive interpretations of situations. These interpretations are then cross-examined and if possible tested out empirically. Thus the client who is distressed at being invited to a party might have a belief of the sort 'I will not be able to handle it, I will not know what to say, I will be so embarrassed'. Beck would negotiate with the client a manageable testing out of this belief (collaborative empiricism) with the counsellor and client agreeing that the client should, say, go to the party late, with a friend and spend most of the time talking to the friend.

4   *Structural cognitive therapy*: In structural cognitive therapy (Liotti, 1986) the concern is with 'deep' structures and three levels of cognitive organisation are posited:

   (a) *Core level*: beliefs (schemata) of the individual that have been formed, usually during childhood and adolescence,

and that are tacitly held by the individual as unques-
tionable assumptions about some important aspect of self
and reality.

(b) *Intermediate level*: verbalisable, explicit descriptions of the
self, other people and the world.

(c) *Peripheral level*: the plans of action and problem solving
strategies that each individual is able to develop in his or
her day-to-day confrontation with the environment.

A primary concern in structural cognitive therapy is to
make explicit the core level. The treatment, for example, of an
agoraphobic client would begin with behavioural strategies of
helping the client to try going gradually greater distances
alone, but therapy would not be terminated when the client
had learned to travel alone. Therapy would also explore
deeper issues such as 'Who am I getting out and about for
anyway?', and examine developmentally linked events such
as frequently having been put on various kinds of transport
as a child to be looked after by a variety of adult carers
because 'Mum wasn't well'.

The time scale for the application of the first three categories of
CBT is brief compared with traditional psychotherapy, typically
involving weekly sessions over three to four months. However,
the time scale for the fourth category, structural cognitive
therapy, is considerably longer, typically 18 months, as its goal is
to achieve fundamental changes in the individual.

Cognitive-behavioural counselling has of late been adapted to
an ever widening range of emotional disorders, personality disorders and problems in living. The advances in practice described
in this text reflect the increasing emphasis on the importance of
considering historical material and recent developments in the
conceptualisation of core disorders and client concerns.

I   Beyond the Basics

1 Appreciate the limitations of the assumptions underlying basic cognitive-behavioural counselling

Young (1994) has pointed out that there are seven assumptions associated with standard brief CBC that may be less than wholly true and particularly so with clients with personality disorders. These are as follows:

1 *That clients have access to their feelings.* Some clients particularly those with longer-term disorders may be blocked and out of touch with what they feel.
2 *That clients have access to thoughts and images.* Many patients with personality disorders cannot report what their automatic thoughts are or they claim not to have images.
3 *That clients have identifiable problems on which to focus.* Some clients may have a general malaise for which they are not able to identify specific triggers.
4 *That clients have the motivation to do homework assignments and learn self-control strategies.* Some clients are more motivated to lean on the counsellor and to obtain support than to learn strategies for helping themselves.
5 *That clients can engage in a collaborative relationship with the counsellor within a few sessions.* Some clients become 'addicted' to the counsellor while others disengage or are hostile.
6 *That difficulties in the therapeutic relationship are not a major problem focus.* For many clients with personality disorders the core of their problem is interpersonal and this is likely to be reflected in the relationship with the counsellor.
7 *That all cognitions and behaviour patterns can be changed through empirical analysis, logical discourse, experimentation, gradual steps and practice.* Some clients insist that their style of thinking and behaviour is so much a part of them that they cannot change at this point in their lives.

Key point

Basic cognitive-behavioural counselling assumes that an individual's distressing interpretations of situations are readily identifiable and can be modified successfully through empirical analysis and experimentation. This may not always be the case!

---

2 Refine your assessment to include a screening for personality disorder

Personality disordered clients, according to the diagnostic criteria in DSM-IV (*Diagnostic and Statistical Manual of Mental Disorders*, 4th edition; American Psychiatric Association, 1994), have to have shown their pathology by early adulthood and, in the case of antisocial personality disorder, some symptoms (for example, conduct disorder) have to have been present before age 15. If it is the case that personality disordered clients are indeed those most likely to violate assumptions 1–7 in the previous section, then traditional assessment has to be refined to take better account of the historical dimension. A personality disorder diagnosis will itself carry counselling implications. Even in cases where a client does not have sufficient symptoms of a particular personality disorder to merit the label, a sub-threshold level of symptoms may do much to illuminate the particular case and its treatment.

The ten personality disorder descriptors in DSM-IV are summarised in Table 2.1 together with some examples of their particular cognitive content.

The personality disorders described in Table 2.1 are not thought by the authors of DSM-IV necessarily to exhaust all possible personality disorder diagnoses, and to cover this they have a category of 'personality disorder not otherwise specified' (PDNOS). This category is provided for two situations: first, the individual's personality pattern meets the general criteria for a personality disorder and traits of several different personality disorders are present, but the criteria for any specific personality

Table 2.1 *DSM-IV summary descriptions of personality disorders and examples of cognitive content*

Cluster A – 'odd'

1 *Paranoid personality disorder* – is a pattern of distrust and suspiciousness such that others' motives are interpreted as malevolent:

- 'Often people deliberately want to annoy me.'
- 'I cannot trust other people.'
- 'It isn't safe to confide in other people.'

2 *Schizoid personality disorder* – is a pattern of detachment from social relationships and a restricted range of emotional expression:

- 'Relationships are messy and interfere with freedom.'
- 'Intimate relations with other people are not important to me.'
- 'I shouldn't confide in others.'

3 *Schizotypal personality disorder* – is a pattern of acute discomfort in close relationships, cognitive or perceptual distortions, and eccentricities of behaviour.
  Cognitive content is much the same as schizoid above.

Cluster B – 'dramatic'

4 *Antisocial personality disorder* – is a pattern of disregard for, and violation of, the rights of others:

- 'Other people are weak and deserve to be taken.'
- 'If I want something I should do whatever is necessary to get it.'
- 'People will get at me if I don't get at them first.'

5 *Borderline personality disorder* – is a pattern of instability in interpersonal relationships, self-image, and affects, coupled with marked impulsivity.
  There is no specific cognitive content but others are regarded as dangerous and malignant, and the self is regarded as being powerless and vulnerable as well as being inherently bad and unacceptable both to the self and to others.

6 *Histrionic personality disorder* – is a pattern of excessive emotionality and attention seeking:

- 'Unless I entertain or impress people, I am nothing.'
- 'I should be the centre of attention.'
- 'People will pay attention only if I act in extreme ways.'

7 *Narcissistic personality disorder* – is a pattern of grandiosity, need for admiration, and lack of empathy:

- 'I don't have to be bound by rules that apply to other people.'
- 'If others don't respect my status they should be punished.'
- 'People have no right to criticise me.'

Continued overleaf

Table 2.1   *(cont.)*

Cluster C – 'anxious'

8   *Avoidant personality disorder* – is a pattern of social inhibition, feelings of inadequacy, and hypersensitivity to negative evaluation:

- 'If people get close to me they will discover the real me and reject me.'
- 'If I think or feel something unpleasant I should try to wipe it out or distract myself.'
- 'Unpleasant feelings will escalate and get out of control.'

9   *Dependent personality disorder* – is a pattern of submissive and clinging behaviour related to an excessive need to be taken care of:

- 'I am needy and weak.'
- 'I need somebody around available at all times to help me carry out what I need to do in case something bad happens.'
- 'I need others to help me make decisions or tell me what to do.'

10   *Obsessive compulsive personality disorder* – is a pattern of preoccupation with orderliness, perfectionism, and control:

- 'It is important to do a perfect job on everything.'
- 'Details are extremely important.'
- 'I have to depend on myself to see that things get done.'

disorder are not met; or, second, the individual's personality pattern meets the general criteria for a personality disorder, but the individual is considered to have a personality disorder that is not included in the current classification (for example, passive-aggressive personality disorder or depressive personality disorder).

Each of the ten descriptions of personality disorders in DMS-IV is followed by a list of features that are the visible expression of that personality disorder. For a personality disorder diagnosis more than a threshold number of features is required. Unfortunately screening a person for all the personality disorders takes at least an hour using an instrument such as the Structured Clinical Interview for Diagnosing Personality Disorders (Spitzer et al., 1990), and is only really appropriate to research contexts. But the concern of the counsellor is not so much with the dichotomy between personality disorder or no personality disorder, but rather with seeing individuals on a continuum of no personality disorder features at one end to all features at the other end. The counsellor's interventions will reflect where on this continuum he or she locates the person. (The cut-off used by researchers is a somewhat arbitrary marker along this continuum.) Individuals who meet criteria for one personality disorder often also meet criteria for one or more others. The ten personality disorder descriptors can be used as yardsticks for profiling the client. It is this profile that the counsellor should be responding to.

As a possible brief rule of thumb as to whether a client has a personality disorder Butler (personal communication) developed the following question:

Rating of Personality Disorder: (To be done after 1st assessment)

Does this person definitely have a personality disorder i.e. their symptoms:

(a) Are characteristic of their long-term functioning and are not limited to episodes; and
(b) Cause significant impairment of social, occupational or personal functioning

Yes/No? (only answer 'Yes' if sure about it).

Using this question 18 per cent of patients referred to psychiatric outpatients had a personality disorder. The first author came up with a similar proportion for patients referred to him in primary care. Of 90 consecutive new referrals 13 per cent had a personality disorder using the Butler question. Of these 90, 62 were generalised anxiety disorder, panic disorder or depression with 14.5 per cent of these having a personality disorder. In an earlier investigation Scott et al. (1994a, 1994b) used the SCID (Structured Clinical Interview for DSM-III-R, 1990) instrument to diagnose personality disorders among patients who met diagnostic criteria for generalised anxiety disorder, panic disorder or depression and found that the proportion with a personality disorder was 50 per cent. The use of the Butler question is, it seems, unlikely to produce any false positives but will likely underestimate the prevalence of personality disorders. Nevertheless it will probably identify those most likely to be refractory to standard cognitive-behavioural counselling. It may be that the Butler question captures those most prototypical of the personality disorders, but there is then a further group who have personality traits that may affect the nature and course of their emotional disorder, and a final group where there are no particular personality traits that affect the onset and course of their emotional disorder. From a clinical point of view thinking in terms of prototypicality might be more useful than the dichotomy of personality disorder versus no personality disorder. This approach is consistent with the finding that personality disorders present as continuous, dimensional, personality traits among healthy subjects and are simply more pronounced in patients with mental disorder (Ekselius et al., 1993).

It appears that a personality disorder diagnosis has a greater significance for the treatment of depressed clients than anxious clients. Scott et al. (1994a, 1994b) found that depressed clients without a personality disorder did significantly better in group cognitive-behavioural counselling than those with a personality disorder whereas for anxious patients (both generalised anxiety disorder and panic disorder clients) there was no significant difference in outcome between those with and without personality disorder. Dreesen et al. (1994) have also reported that personality disorders do not influence the results of cognitive-behaviour therapies for anxiety disorders. It remains to be established whether a diagnosis of personality disorder affects outcome in other disorders such as bulimia nervosa.

Not all personality disorders are likely to be of equal relevance in terms of outcome. In the two studies noted above if patients had a coexisting personality disorder it was usually a cluster C 'anxious' personality disorder (which are the most common personality disorder diagnoses) and the results probably more reflect comparisons between those with and without a cluster C personality disorder. Intuitively it seems likely that there will be particularly marked differences for those with and without cluster A and cluster B personality disorders because they show the most marked deviations from normal personality. Some indication of this is provided in the Scott et al. (1994b) study in that among clients treated for depression there was a significant difference in the proportion of clients with and without a borderline personality disorder who engaged in an adequate 'dose' of therapy. Further studies are however required to demonstrate the particular relevance of cluster A and cluster B diagnoses. It may also be the case that even for patients with anxiety disorder there will be a difference between those with a severe cluster C personality disorder and those with moderate versus mild versus no personality disorder but again this awaits empirical investigation.

Scott et al. (1994a, 1994b) found that brief group cognitive therapy was effective with both depressed and generalised anxiety disorder clients except for clients with a coexisting personality disorder. Nevertheless, the group format for those with a concurrent personality disorder may still be as good an option because there is little evidence that individual counselling is any better for this population, though the group format does restrict the flexibility of approach that is typically necessary with the personality disordered. A case can be made for a group intervention with the personality disordered but as part of a stepped care programme in which group intervention is supplemented with individual sessions.

Historically the focus of cognitive-behaviour therapy has been primarily on symptom reduction and this led to the development of brief programmes, usually of three months or less, for disorders such as depression or anxiety. The results of outcome studies have shown that typically 75 per cent of clients have responded to these programmes. This indicates that symptom reduction is often an achievable target for most anxious and depressed clients within a three-month period. In a summary of the literature relating client variables to outcome, Prochaska and DiClemente (1984) found that lower levels of defensiveness, less externalisation of blame, the presence of felt emotional pain such as anxiety or depression and positive expectations for counselling all bore positive relationships to treatment outcome. It seems likely that the non-responders to these brief programmes had particularly pervasive maladaptive personality traits and indeed those who relapsed subsequently may perhaps have had at least some sub-threshold level of personality disorder. The consensus seems to be that effective treatment of clients with personality disorders takes one and a half to four years. Thus the duration of treatment is likely to be in a range from 2–3 months to 1.5–4 years depending on the pervasiveness of the patient's maladaptive personality traits.

Many of those with personality disorders have experienced multiple episodes of traumatic abuse of varying types by adults in childhood and it may therefore be useful to treat these clients as victims of trauma. The duration of therapy will also be influenced by whether the client exists in a therapeutically benign or hostile environment. An asymptomatic depressive, for example, has been found to be much more likely to relapse if returning to an environment in which there are high levels of criticism and over-involvement, such as where there are high levels of expressed emotion (Hooley et al., 1986). The ability to engage clients in treatment in the first place is also influenced by the nature of the personality disorders involved. In clients meeting DSM-IV diagnostic criteria for anxiety and depression, approximately 50 per cent of them have personality disorders in the 'anxious' cluster C category and they are much easier to engage than say, heroin addicts, many of whom have a 'dramatic' cluster B personality disorder.

Realistically it may not be possible to work with certain personality disordered clients, for example those who truly lack empathy for others, fail to experience remorse over their actions, and/or habitually externalise their actions. As Bedrosian and Bozicas (1994) suggest, some measure of dissatisfaction with oneself seems to be a necessary precondition for counselling.

Key point

The DSM-IV diagnostic criteria for personality disorders should be borne in mind when assessing clients. The presence of a coexisting personality disorder may influence the efficacy of basic cognitive-behavioural counselling for depression.

---

3   Explore the client's pre-adult functioning and determine the appropriateness of a personality disorder classification

The essence of the cognitive-behavioural model is that clients' strains (anxiety, depression, and so on) are influenced by their perceptions of stressors (becoming unemployed, being abused, and so on). In an attempt to reduce the strains the client then uses various coping strategies. At a first interview clients will usually easily volunteer information on any current stressors, but are less precise about their strains and point to the inadequacy of their coping strategies. The unwary counsellor can, however, take the current stressors as a given without realising that, in large measure, it is a particular perception of the stressor that gives rise to the distress. A model of clients' current difficulties should therefore include information under the following headings:

- Stressors
- Strains
- Thoughts and images about stressors
- Coping strategies.

These features encompass the current destabilisation of the client. Certain stressors are more likely to be associated with particular strains – loss with depression, threat with anxiety, extraordinary stressors outside the normal range of human experience with post-traumatic stress disorder. The focus of brief cognitive-behavioural counselling is on the development of a more accurate perception of the stressor and the evolution of a more adaptive coping strategy. Stressors may be of low magnitude occurring individually or cumulatively. Examples of low magnitude stressors would include job loss, financial difficulties, marital difficulties, breaking up with significant others, divorce or separation, serious illness of self or family member, and death of a relative or close friend. However, low magnitude stressors should not be thought of as necessarily synonymous with events but can also include being placed in positions of role conflict or ambiguity, or of 'demand overload'. Intuitively, clients whose distress is a product of relatively low magnitude stressors of recent origin are likely to be much easier to treat than those subjected to high magnitude stressors now and possibly also in childhood. Indeed the success of brief cognitive-behavioural counselling may in part be a result of treating patients who have for the most part experienced low magnitude stressors comparatively recently. When clients indicate that their distress goes back to early adulthood or they are unresponsive to treatment, it is important to enquire about childhood and adolescent stressors.

The pro forma in Table 3.1 can be used to collect data on pre-adulthood functioning. Very disturbed clients may have experienced high magnitude stressors which might include severe physical punishment (child abuse), sexual abuse, experiencing the homicide of a close friend or family member, witnessing someone seriously injured or killed, or experiencing a natural disaster. The data from the pre-adult functioning table can be used to trace the evolution of clients' views of themselves, their personal world and their strategies for interacting with the world. While each client's triad – that is, view of self, world and coping strategy – is unique, there are family resemblances between triads to the point that particular combinations appear to describe particular personality disorders. Forgus and Shulman (1979) have suggested core syllogisms for some of the personality disorders, for example for obsessive-compulsive personality they suggest:

- 'I am liable to be held responsible for what goes wrong.'
- 'Life is unpredictable.'
- 'Therefore I have to guard against anything that might go wrong.'

Table 3.1 *Pre-adult functioning*

	0–4	5–10	11–16	17–21
Stressors				
Strains				
Thoughts/images				
Coping strategies				

A comprehensive understanding of a client's difficulties may therefore require attention to both current stressors and historical material, and the latter may reveal particular vulnerabilities. For example the current stressor for a client might be work overload and the client's history might indicate an overriding perfectionism (vulnerability). These two factors may interact to produce great distress – the client literally not having the time to do things perfectly. The perfectionism itself may have developed as the adolescent attempt to compensate for feelings of inadequacy following a rape. Indeed this person would likely have an obsessive-compulsive personality disorder.

Key point

Extreme stressors in childhood are likely to make individuals vulnerable to the development of personality disorders. Particular combinations of the triad 'I am . . . ', 'Life is . . . ', 'Therefore I . . . ' tend to describe specific personality disorders.

---

4   Draw and share your conceptualisation of the client's difficulties

Drawing and sharing your conceptualisation of the client's difficulties gives the client a map of how he or she arrived at the present position, and also opens up the possibility that alternative routes could have been taken if the client had known then what he or she knows now. To take an example, Elaine was referred for counselling for a depression which had been of varying intensities, but had persisted ever since she could remember. The present trigger for the depressive episode was her best friend's partner making a pass at her. The counsellor asked her when was the first time that she could remember feeling as bad as she did at present. Elaine replied that it was when she started at school and other children avoided her because she had psoriasis. She also remembered attending the doctor and adults ushering their children away from her. Finally a picture was drawn of her difficulties, shown in Figure 4.1.

Elaine had developed an avoidant personality disorder and in an attempt to put herself beyond the criticism of others she was very perfectionist and also met the diagnostic criteria for obsessive-compulsive personality disorder.

From Figure 4.1 it can be seen that Elaine's constant view of herself was that she was flawed, defective and unlovable and other people were cruel and harsh. As she had gone through her life she had collected further evidence that confirmed (schema maintenance) her negative view of herself, for example under-achieving at school. On the one hand she berated herself for staying in abusive relationships longer than she believed a 'proper person' should, but had not realised that this had been because she regarded herself as 'Less than a person'. In work she readily agreed to tasks that were under-resourced to secure the approval of her bosses. As a consequence she had become totally exhausted.

Tackling a client's earliest maladaptive interpretation (EMI) of a situation represents an evolution of cognitive-behaviour therapy in which historical material is treated with the same respect as the

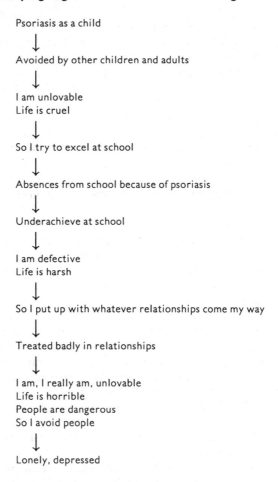

Psoriasis as a child

↓

Avoided by other children and adults

↓

I am unlovable
Life is cruel

↓

So I try to excel at school

↓

Absences from school because of psoriasis

↓

Underachieve at school

↓

I am defective
Life is harsh

↓

So I put up with whatever relationships come my way

↓

Treated badly in relationships

↓

I am, I really am, unlovable
Life is horrible
People are dangerous
So I avoid people

↓

Lonely, depressed

Figure 4.1   *Elaine's difficulties*

current data of the client's experience. The EMI can be located by applying a 'But for . . . ' criterion. In the case of Elaine as described in Figure 4.1, 'But for' her initial interpretation that other children's avoidance of her meant that she was unlovable, she would not subsequently have endured destructive relationships for such long periods. A confirmatory bias is a universal phenomenon, in that once a person takes a view of him- or herself in relation to his or her social world that person more actively processes information that confirms this view and is inclined to discount information that is discrepant with it. Thus

Elaine saw her adult relationships with men as confirming her unlovability and discounted her good relationships with her parents, brother and one or two friends on the grounds that they 'just happened to be particularly nice people'. Thus she came to meet the diagnostic criteria for avoidant personality disorder.

However, the EMI does not necessarily apply to a childhood phenomenon, it is simply the interpretation surrounding the first major trauma. Gloria, for example, had experienced no emotional difficulties until she suffered depression following the break-up of her marriage. The marriage she thought had been an excellent one until her husband suddenly left her for another woman. She had concluded from this experience that 'You cannot rely on anything'.

When the EMIs have taken place in childhood they have then been subjected to a long period of operation of the confirmatory bias, becoming the operational 'commandments' for organising oneself with regard to the world and to relationships in particular. EMIs in adulthood typically have not been 'fed' as long and often have more of the status of 'guidelines' for action than 'commandments'. 'Commandments' (which are the particular property of personality disordered individuals) are much more likely to be refractory to treatment than 'guidelines'. It should be remembered that these commandments and guidelines are also a socially constructed phenomenon and that their permeability will in part depend on their validation or otherwise by significant others in the client's life.

The EMI is formed in the context of a particular audience. The reactions of this audience are used subsequently as a template, as to how other audiences will respond, that is, the person may carry with him or her the early maladaptive expectations of others (EMEOs). A focus on the EMEOs with depressed personality disordered clients parallels the focus on the client's negative view of the world in traditional cognitive therapy. The EMEOs lead to a filtering of experiences with audiences so that evidence confirming the expectation is more centrally processed and evidence that might disconfirm the EMEO is more peripherally processed. In peripheral processing, the content of the experience is not critically examined, rather simple rules of thumb operate. For example, Jean was abused in childhood and developed an EMI that she must be seriously flawed to have had this experience, and her EMEO was that others would abuse her given the opportunity. Subsequently she met John who began courting her, but his various acts of kindness were summarily dismissed with her rule of thumb 'He must be after something', confirming the

EMEO and leaving unchallenged the EMI. Thus a confirmatory bias serves to maintain the EMI and EMEO. In the more severely personality disordered clients like Jean the defence of the EMI and EMEO can become extreme, and she would taunt and physically assault her boyfriend in an attempt to provoke him into attacking and just using her, thereby providing confirmation. Thus the therapeutic targets with Jean, and similarly personality disordered depressed clients, are on the clients' current coping strategies (CCS), early maladaptive interpretations of self (EMIS) and early maladaptive expectations of others (EMEOs).

The interpersonal aspects of the client's life should also be a prime target. Where possible a family member, partner or friend should be encouraged to take on the role of quasi-therapist. Consideration should also be given to the possibility of engaging the client in group therapy to help counteract the idea that he or she is cut-off or apart from the rest of the human race. Encouraging clients to engage with others allows them to actually test out their beliefs that, for example, they will always be rejected by others.

Key point

Drawing and sharing your conceptualisation of the client's difficulties with the client illustrates to him or her how information has been continuously processed to confirm initial negative interpretations of the client and his or her world. It also highlights the arbitrariness of the client's initial interpretations. The client's earliest maladaptive interpretations of self (EMIS) can be identified by the 'But for . . .' technique and is a prime therapeutic target as is the client's early maladaptive expectations of others (EMEOs).

5 Explain to the client that he or she may be the victim of adults with personality disorders

A client's difficulties may sometimes best be conceptualised as a product of the traumas enacted by others with personality disorders, particularly cluster A and cluster B disorders. This traumatisation may occur in childhood at the hands of adults but it can also often be observed in couples where one partner has a cluster A or cluster B personality disorder. Individuals with a cluster A or cluster B disorder will rarely present for or stay in counselling, but educating the client about the nature of the partner's or parent's disorder can do much to counter excessive self-blame, which is an inevitable concomitant of depression. The main strategies of the personality disordered are summarised in Table 5.1 (taken from Beck et al. 1990, pp. 54–5).

The strategies of the personality disordered are likely to have deleterious effects on many of their significant others. In the case of children with a personality disordered parent they may struggle valiantly to accept the legitimacy of the parental strategy as not to do so would risk accepting that they did not have a caring reliable adult as a parent and risk the consequent feelings of abandonment. The child may begin to experience guilt as he or she begins to doubt the legitimacy of the parental behaviours, or alternatively the child may begin to imitate the personality disordered strategy he or she sees. In working with adult survivors of personality disordered parents it is important to increase and legitimise intolerance of the parental strategy.

Key point

Clients may be the victims of strategies employed by personality disordered adults. Explaining this to a client can sometimes lessen the client's excessive self-blame.

Table 5.1 *Main strategies of particular personality disorders*

Personality disorder	Main strategies
Avoidant	Avoid evaluative situations Avoid unpleasant feelings or thoughts
Dependent	Cultivate dependent relationships
Passive-aggressive	Passive resistance Surface submissiveness Evade, circumvent rules
Obsessive-compulsive	Apply rules Perfectionism Criticise Punish
Paranoid	Be wary Look for hidden motives Accuse Counterattack
Antisocial	Attack Rob Deceive Manipulate
Narcissistic	Use others Transcend rules Manipulate Compete
Histrionic	Use dramatics, charm Temper tantrums, crying Suicide gestures
Schizoid	Stay away

6 Use the following guidelines in treating all personality disordered clients

Although there are a variety of cognitive-behavioural approaches to the counselling of the personality disordered client there is nevertheless a consensus that it is important to follow the guidelines distilled by Flemming and Pretzer (1990), which are summarised in Table 6.1. It should be emphasised however that none of the CB approaches for treating personality disorders have yet been empirically evaluated.

The concepts of EMIS and EMEO provide a framework for idiosyncratic and individual conceptualizations of the self. A complementary approach, suggested by Young (1994), is to posit a finite range of schemas (in his case 16) one or more of which account for the distress of any individual. He groups these under the following five headings:

1 *Disconnection and rejection*: expectation that one's needs for security, safety, stability, nurturance, empathy, sharing of feelings, acceptance and respect will not be met in a predictable manner.
2 *Impaired autonomy and performance*: expectations about oneself and the environment that interfere with one's perceived ability to separate, survive, function independently or perform successfully.
3 *Impaired limits*: deficiency in internal limits, responsibility to others, or long-term goal orientation. Leads to difficulty respecting the rights of others, making commitments, or setting and meeting personal goals.
4 *Other-directedness*: an excessive focus on the desires, feelings and responses of others at the expense of one's own needs, in order to gain love and approval, maintain one's sense of connection, or avoid retaliation.
5 *Overvigilance and inhibition*: excessive emphasis on controlling one's spontaneous feelings, impulses and choices in order to avoid making mistakes or on meeting rigid, internalised rules and expectations about performance and ethical behaviour,

Table 6.1 *Guidelines for counselling clients with personality disorders*

1 Interventions are most effective when based on an individualised conceptualisation of the client's problems.
2 It is important for the counsellor and client to work collaboratively towards clearly identified shared goals.
3 It is important to focus more than usual attention on the counsellor–client interaction.
4 Consider interventions that do not require extensive client self-disclosure.
5 Interventions which increase the client's sense of self-efficacy often reduce the intensity of the client's symptomatology and facilitate other interventions.
6 The counsellor should not rely primarily on verbal interventions.
7 The counsellor should try to identify and address the client's fears before implementing changes.
8 The counsellor should anticipate problems with compliance.
9 The counsellor should not assume that the client exists in a reasonable or functional environment.
10 The counsellor must attend to his or her emotional reactions during the course of therapy.
11 The counsellor should be realistic regarding the length of therapy, goals for therapy, and standards for self evaluation.

Source: Flemming and Pretzer (1990)

often at the expense of happiness, self-expression, relaxation, close relationships or health.

Perhaps the biggest shift in emphasis from basic cognitive-behavioural counselling to that designed for the personality disordered client is in the emphasis on the therapeutic relationship. In traditional cognitive-behaviour therapy the counsellor's own emotional reactions to the client are not accorded particular significance. By contrast, with the personality disordered client the client's impact on the counsellor may provide useful data as to how the client may be affecting significant others. It may well be that the client's current negative feedback from significant others is a major concern. Of course a pre-condition for the counsellor disclosing to the client the latter's impact is that they have been made to feel safe in the therapeutic environment.

Key point

With personality disordered clients the status of the therapeutic relationship is raised. Specifically the client's transactions with the counsellor are seen as a microcosm of the client's interactions with the outside world.

---

7   Consider the use of groups

Counsellors have to consider that those procedures which are the most effective may not necessarily be the most efficient and this may be of prime importance in an audit of the counsellor's work. Counselling does not exist in a vacuum, a format of therapy that is very effective may not be viable because it is very labour intensive. The prime concern of sources of referral (who may also be the paymasters) is more likely to be with counsellor efficiency – that is, the mean percentage change on some measure for patients with a particular disorder divided by the time needed to achieve this change – than with whether the counsellor can ultimately bring about change with the most difficult of patients. The traditional choice of 15–20 individual therapy sessions over a three-month period can look very different from the vantage point of counsellor efficiency. For example in Table 7.1 the efficiency of different modalities for depression is contrasted. The formula used for counsellor efficiency was mean percentage change on the Beck Depression Inventory divided by the amount of counsellor time needed to achieve the change per client.

From Table 7.1 it can be seen that the important differences in terms of efficiency are not the differing counselling schools, with ratings of 4–5, but between individual modalities and group interventions. The Scott and Stradling (1990) study showed that group and individual therapy for depression were equally *effective*, in terms of amount of change effected *per* patient, and thus that group delivery of treatment, requiring less therapist time *per* patient, was considerably more efficient. This finding has been replicated in a study by Zettle et al. (1992) who compared the efficacy of 12 weekly sessions of group cognitive therapy with the same number of individual sessions. A particularly interesting aspect of the Zettle et al. study was that clients did best in the treatment format that matched their personality. Thus clients whose identity was very much bound up with achievement did better in individual therapy while those for whom the approval of others was very important did better in group therapy. This suggests that matching clients to counselling format may be an

Table 7.1 *Counsellor efficiency*

	Efficiency score
Scott and Stradling (1990) – a 12-session group programme with up to 3 individual sessions initially	14.52
Scott et al. (1994b) – 7-session group programme plus an individual session 'If you really need it'	13.33
Williams (1992) – review of individual cognitive therapy outcome studies (total time 12.75 hours per client assuming 17 sessions at 45 mins per session)	5.25
Nietzel (1987) – other individual psychotherapeutic modalities, assuming 17 sessions	4.31

important step towards better targeting the efficient deployment of therapist effort.

At the moment the jury is still out as to whether group cognitive-behaviour therapy is as effective as individual cognitive-behaviour therapy for disorders such as generalised anxiety disorder, panic disorder and bulimia nervosa. But given the ever lengthening waiting lists within the UK NHS, the burden of proof should perhaps rest with those who would make a case for the supremacy of individual therapy.

Probably the overriding characteristic of clients with personality disorders is that they have severe interpersonal difficulties. To some degree they may overcome these difficulties in their relationship with the counsellor who in individual counselling may provide a limited form of re-parenting. However, the results may not generalise from the relationship with the counsellor, who may easily be dismissed by a rule of thumb such as 'They are a one-off'. It becomes more difficult however to dismiss a group of people as wholly atypical. Group cognitive-behavioural counselling has been conducted with avoidant personality disorder clients. Alden (1989) showed that avoidant patients who participated in a ten week group treatment programme displayed significantly greater improvement on a variety of self-report and behavioural measures than did untreated controls. However, these avoidant subjects were not functioning at the level of normative comparison samples at treatment termination. It should

Table 7.2 *Guidelines for groupwork*

1 Carefully market the group and decide what, if any, supplementary individual sessions need to be provided.
2 Use homogeneous groups.
3 Have a co-leader if possible.
4 Have a session-by-session plan of material to be covered plus appropriate handouts.
5 Have clients model effective use of the skills.
6 Problem solve the difficulties of unsuccessful group members.
7 Use the group to draw similarities between members' difficulties to lessen their sense of isolation.
8 Ensure you don't lose individual group members by carefully tailoring homework assignments and making sure that you review each individual's progress.

also be borne in mind that clients with a clinically significant depressive component were excluded from the study. Alden recommended that longer periods of treatment be evaluated. The group counselling involved: (1) identifying the fears underlying the avoidant pattern (for example, a fear of being negatively evaluated); (2) increasing awareness of the anxiety-producing effects of dwelling on such fears; and (3) shifting attentional focus from fear-related thinking to behavioural action.

There are certain caveats to be borne in mind when conducting groupwork and these are summarised in Table 7.2.

Key point

Group cognitive-behavioural counselling can be as efficacious as individual counselling and may be a more efficient use of counselling resources. Very autonomous depressed clients may do better in individual counselling while those very dependent on the approval of others may do better in group counselling. There are particular advantages in having personality disordered clients in a group modality at some point in their counselling. Certain guidelines need to be observed in conducting groupwork.

II Depression

8 Activate and focus depressed clients

The characteristic mode of the depressed client is to be inactive, and this current coping strategy (CCS) itself often becomes a source of guilt, thereby compounding the depression. The depressed client's rationale for the inactivity is often a thought such as 'I am not going to enjoy it so why bother'. The first stage of Beck's cognitive therapy is to monitor activity by requiring the client to record on a scale from 1 to 10 the sense of achievement and pleasure derived from activities during the day. The data recorded are then used to point out that the client in fact seems to feel better during some activities and that this might be capitalised on by scheduling in more of such activities, particularly for identified low spots during the day. The activity schedules almost always show variations in mood and this should be highlighted to challenge a belief common to depressives that they are 'Always low'. The timetabling in of potentially uplifting events by the client carries with it an implicit assumption that the client is able to influence his or her mood and begins to act as an antidote to the sense of helplessness.

A prime target in traditional cognitive therapy for depression is the client's negative self-view. With the depressed personality disordered client the focus needs to shift slightly to the early maladaptive interpretation of self (EMIS). The therapeutic targets for personality disordered depressed clients are current coping strategies (CCS), early maladaptive interpretations of self (EMIS), and early maladaptive expectations of others (EMEO). The EMIS and EMEO can, however, be elusive targets because during both their determination and subsequent re-appraisal the client may move discussion of them on to some current but less highly charged life crisis, that is, the client employs cognitive avoidance.

With Jean, for example, the counsellor often found that they ran out of time during sessions to work sufficiently on them. This cognitive avoidance is usually matched by the use of behavioural avoidance as one of the client's current coping strategies – for example Jean would not sit next to men on buses. As the counsellor becomes more aware of the client's cognitive avoidance, it becomes easier to impose a timetable for the discussion of sensitive material. In order to be able to do this, however, the counsellor has to pay more than usual attention to the quality of the therapeutic relationship and especially to establishing rapport. Even when a timetable for the discussion of sensitive issues is agreed, the client may engage in further avoidance behaviour of which the counsellor may not be entirely aware. Jean would often complain of the temperature of the room and lack of ventilation and would dig her nails into her arm and hurt herself when discussing her sexual relationship with her partner. Thus cognitive and behavioural avoidance are obstacles to be surmounted in addressing the targets. Indeed the severity of avoidance, both cognitive and behavioural, is often a reflection of the severity of personality disorder. Emotional avoidance may be a further obstacle to addressing the targets, for example Jean berated her sister for not making a long pilgrimage across town to visit their father's grave on the anniversary of his death. He had abused both of them.

Cognitive and behavioural avoidance can be tackled by challenging their utility. The client can be asked whether the refusal to think through the highly charged issues by blocking them off has worked for the client – their presence in counselling can be used as data that avoidance has been ultimately counter-productive. Having the client list the advantages and disadvantages, both short and long term, of addressing the avoided material can help the latter to use central processing during counselling. Typically clients have concentrated on the short-term pain of addressing highly charged material rather than the long-term gain – in this context it can be useful to draw an analogy with the withdrawal problems of cigarette cessation and the long-term health benefits. However, in order to make the decision to address hitherto avoided material clients need space, and a considered decision is likely to prove more stable than one made in haste or under pressure from the counsellor. A precondition for addressing such material is that the client feels safe with the counsellor, and again with the personality disordered client the relationship aspects of counselling loom larger than with counselling those without a personality disorder.

The counsellor's ability to make the client feel safe will vary from personality disorder to personality disorder. At one extreme the counsellor can easily make the depressed client with a dependent personality disorder feel too safe, and at the other extreme a client with an avoidant personality is likely to be hypersensitive to any hint of criticism or rejection.

> **Key point**
>
> Have the depressed client structure his or her day so as to engage in potential uplifts. The utility of the client's avoidance of highly charged material can be challenged by suggesting they consider the advantages and disadvantages of such behaviour both short and long term.

9 Use the data of the therapeutic relationship to illustrate points

Personality disorder features will be manifested in the interaction with the counsellor. Thus the dependent personality disordered client may well complain, for example, about the length of the counsellor's holiday and the delay before the next appointment. Whereas the counsellor arriving five minutes late for an appointment with an avoidant personality disordered client may find he or she has a client smouldering with resentment. The client with obsessive-compulsive personality disorder may become very irritated by the counsellor's inability to find appointment cards or by a telephone interruption to the interview. In such situations the thought processes that underlie the various 'anxious' (cluster C) personality disorders become more evident than in the typical cognitive therapy Socratic dialogue, that is they are 'hot', and it is therefore very important that they are used to challenge the client's habitual style.

It should be noted that the differing anxious personality disorders require of the counsellor a different style. With the dependent personality disorder the counsellor is somewhat distant but encouraging; with the avoidant personality disorder the counsellor may make a point of being particularly available, for example, by giving an out-of-hours telephone number; while with the obsessive-compulsive the counsellor may model a balanced life-style albeit with some disorganisation which never proves catastrophic. In this way the counsellor uses his or her office manner to some degree to bring about change in the client's EMIS and EMEO.

Unfortunately it is much less clear what counselling style should be adopted with clients with the 'odd' (cluster A) personality disorders. They typically regard relationships in general as messy and unnecessary, and it is therefore extremely difficult to get even to first base with this group. The position with clients with 'dramatic' (cluster B) personality disorders is only marginally better. However, Linehan et al. (1991) have managed to provide a treatment for borderline personality disordered women that was effective in that it significantly reduced para-suicidal behaviours, though not levels of depression, compared with treatment as usual in the community. Her counselling programme involved weekly individual and group therapy sessions for a year, something which is likely to be beyond the resources of the UK NHS on a routine basis. Of these very disturbed clients 83 per cent remained in the counselling programme for the year. Given the success of the Salkovskis et al. (1990) brief problem solving therapy with para-suicidal clients it is possible that this might be as effective as the labour intensive Linehan Programme with borderline personality disordered clients. Beck et al. (1990) have suggested that the way forward with antisocial personality disordered clients is to identify with their life goals but to suggest more efficient and socially acceptable means of achieving these goals. This approach has an intuitive validity but it is still extremely difficult to engage these clients in treatment and where they have been engaged it is usually because of some legal mandate. Clients with the other cluster B personality disorders, narcissistic and histrionic, rarely present voluntarily for counselling as they have no self-dissatisfaction but their significant others may well present as victims suffering from depression. It is perhaps fortuitous that the most prevalent personality disorders among depressed clients are the 'anxious' cluster ones.

Key point

Anticipate that when the counsellor acts as a stimulus for arousing negative emotions in the client the salient dysfunctional thought processes and beliefs of the client have likely been primed. Adopt a counselling style that serves to contradict these evoked maladaptive beliefs.

---

10 Show the client how to track and modify their thoughts

The second stage in Beck's cognitive therapy for depression is more overtly cognitive, during which clients are asked to monitor upsetting situations, note their emotional state, and identify their automatic thoughts – that is, what it seems as if they had said to themselves to make them feel the way they did. Finally clients have to determine a rational response to the automatic thought.

Clients are also encouraged to test out the validity of their negative automatic thought by conducting experiments, a process which Beck terms collaborative empiricism. For example a client unsure about being able to cope at a social function would be encouraged to test out his or her negative predictions by going to the occasion. In this way negative predictions are treated as hypotheses to be tested rather than as facts. This makes the therapy very relevant to the current issues in the client's life. However, the difficulties encountered by the depressed personality disordered client in distilling a rational response and translating it into an adaptive and healthy coping strategy are considerable and seem to necessitate some simultaneous focus on historical material. To facilitate this dual focus on the present and past the pro forma in Table 10.1 may be used. (The authors are indebted to Jeffrey Young for providing the inspiration for this material.)

The focus in the first four steps of the managing distress process in Table 10.1 is on the analysis of current distress. In step 5 the client attempts to put the current strain in a wider context and looks for basic assumptions that may link his or her distress in a variety of situations. A client's ability to do step 5 often depends on having done steps 1–4 for a variety of stressors, thus initially completion of steps 5–8 should be described to the client as a bonus.

Step 6 is particularly important for depressed clients with a personality disorder who often have a developmental deficit manifested in an inability to take on board the perspective of others, and in this sense they are often egocentric. During adolescence the child first acknowledges that, theoretically, others

Table 10.1   *Managing distress*

1 *Triggers*: (What set off my reactions?)
2 *Emotions*: (What was I feeling?)
3 *Thoughts*: (What was I thinking?)
4 *Behaviours*: (What did I actually do?)
5 *Basic assumptions*: (What irrational beliefs of mine might be related?)
6 *Realistic concerns*: (In what ways were my reactions justified? What did I do to cause or worsen the situation?)
7 *Overreactions*: (In what ways did I exaggerate or misinterpret? What did I do to cause or worsen the situation?)
8 *Healthy management*: (In what ways could I cope better in the future or solve the problem?)

may take a view of a situation that differs from his or her own, then the adolescent may go on to learn to check the gut reaction that views differing from his or her own are simply 'Stupid'. The intrapersonal developmental correlate is that the individual comes to see personal views as provisional and 'best guesses under the circumstances'. This involves the development of a tolerance of ambiguity, something which is often noticeably absent among depressed clients.

In steps 7 and 8 the client is encouraged to develop a more balanced view of distress. The acknowledgement of realistic concerns in step 7 can help the client overcome emotional avoidance, and legitimises the expression of negative affect. It also puts the client's plight in an environmental context and suggests that modifications of, say, an overly critical or overly involved significant other's behaviour may be as much a therapeutic target as intrapsychic changes in the client. In step 8 the client is looking to the future and distilling how it is possible to think and behave differently – that is, the client's new coping strategies.

Key point

Teach the client how to detect the influence of current and past thought processes in the development of his or her distress. Remember that it is as valid an intervention to modify a client's toxic environment as to change the client's thought processes.

---

11 Modify early maladaptive interpretations of self and early maladaptive expectations of others

Working with EMIS and EMEO is particularly indicated when the client reports always having been depressed. Further examination of the client's history in age bands usually reveals times of transition, points before which the client was, at least, not aware of being depressed. It is necessary to get the client to concretise the events surrounding these points of transition, as unless this is done the full range of emotions and thought processes surrounding the transition may not be accessed and premature conclusions about EMIS and EMEO may be drawn.

For example, Penny told the counsellor that she did not remember feeling depressed before her mother died when she was seven. To concretise the experience the counsellor asked her to describe her home after her mother died. In a matter of fact manner she described the acquisition of new furniture and then went on to describe her father's fury at the unexpected arrival of a room divider ordered by her maternal grandmother who lived with them. At the mention of the maternal grandmother Penny burst into tears. It transpired that the maternal grandmother had largely reared her as her parents were preoccupied running their shop and attending the local church social club. The salient traumatic event in fact occurred four years later when the maternal grandmother moved away and Penny subsequently saw her only once or twice a month. Her father continued to be preoccupied with his business but after his wife's death developed a drink problem. At school she remembered being embarrassed telling a teacher that she did not have anyone to come up to school for parents' evening. To concretise matters again the counsellor asked what she was thinking and feeling when she came away from the encounter with the teacher and she replied 'Nobody can be bothered with me' (her EMEO) and 'I am not worth bothering about' (EMIS). Potential traumatic incidents should be examined in terms of the actions and goals of the individual rather than their objectively traumatic nature. Thus the incident in which Penny had to tell her teacher that there was not anybody available to come for parents' evening was traumatic because her goal was to feel accepted in school particularly by her teachers, and much of her out-of-school activity was devoted to getting her homework right. The delineation of the client's actions and goals at the time of occurrence of events is as important as the concrete description of those events. It is the initial thwarting of the client's actions and goals that is likely to mark the onset of a depressive episode.

The events around which early maladaptive interpretations are made are necessarily highly subjective, the individual rarely has the opportunity to seek out consensus views on what happened, and the developmental level of the individual means that only a limited range of interpretations could have been considered. The client narrating these events in counselling is likely to accord them a status of absolute truth yet they are, literally, imports from a previous time zone. This should not be taken to mean that the counsellor does not believe the client but that more comprehensive explanations from the vantage point of an adult can be canvassed.

Data furnished about the functioning of siblings may be used to help the client develop a more critical stance about his or her own EMISs and EMEOs. Often there is at least one sibling who manifests similar EMISs and EMEOs and is, or has been, depressed. If the client has a positive regard for the sibling the client is not threatened by being asked to trace the development and operation of the brother's or sister's EMISs and EMEOs. The next stage is to have the client critically examine the validity of the sibling's EMISs and EMEOs and the difficulties experienced in trying to challenge the brother's or sister's negative self-view and of others. This helps clients raise major question marks over their own EMISs and EMEOs as the case of Marian illustrates.

Marian was suffering from severe depression and also from panic attacks. Marian and her brother were regularly physically abused by their father and she formed an EMIS that nobody would ever bother with wanting to know her and an EMEO that she would be abused if she let them get close. She had decided not to have any children 'Because I could not bear them to go through what I have been through' and as a consequence she had had two abortions to which she was morally opposed. At work she was valued by colleagues and had a couple of very close female friends. Her marriage broke down after a year because of her husband's continual violence, this latter experience serving to confirm both her EMIS and her EMEO. Initially the EMIS and EMEO were addressed by asking Marian to write for homework on one side of paper the case for her prosecution and on the other side to spend time on elaborating the case for her defence, then to imagine the deliberations of the jury, and finally whether they would return a 'Guilty', 'Not guilty' or 'Not proven' verdict.

Unfortunately Marian did not complete the exercise as she came to a full stop after she had written two lines of the case for her defence, illustrating how difficult it is for the depressed to access positive information about themselves and others. Her pressing concern at that moment was that her brother was having to come and live with her because his marriage too had broken down, after 18 years, he was depressed and he had nowhere else to go. Marian felt that it might all be beyond her resources and she needed space for herself. She found the break-up of her brother's marriage particularly upsetting as she always thought that he had the one good relationship and she was fond of her brother. The counsellor asked how her brother would probably have written the case for his prosecution and the case for his defence. Marian replied that her brother had always felt inferior to his fellow teachers and didn't think much of himself. When asked how this had come about when he was a headteacher, Marian replied that he had always blamed himself for not facing up to his father because he was supposed to be a male after all. The counsellor then asked what verdict her brother would expect a jury to return on him and Marian replied 'Guilty'. Marian was then asked what verdict she would return on him and she replied 'He's lovely'. As a homework exercise she was asked to write the case for her brother's defence and after writing it attempt to write again the case for her defence. While positive views of and interactions with siblings provide a port of entry into challenging EMISs, so too may non-negative interactions with significant others in the present. Supportive relationships with significant others can be used to suggest that the client has 'developed a prejudice' against him- or herself. Further, the client can be asked to describe interactions with someone who was racially or religiously bigoted to see how information is selectively attended to, and how biases are maintained.

John was 52, severely depressed, and had been out of work for ten years. His wife and children were very supportive but John nevertheless considered himself a failure. When asked how long he had been depressed he replied 'Always!'. The counsellor began an examination of his functioning pre-school and in his primary school and in fact he could report no adverse experiences in these periods. At age 11, however, he passed an examination to go to the grammar school, and this transition proved extremely difficult as he came from a working-class background, none of his friends had passed the examination, and he was mocked for so doing. At school he remembered being highly embarrassed that he only ever had jam sandwiches for lunch and was derided for this by other children. He was dismayed to find that he now struggled with his lessons when previously he had always been near the top of his class. His friends in school were the misfits and he did not socialise with them outside school because of the distance he would have had to travel by public transport. At work after leaving school he refused any challenges because he felt that he would not be able to cope with the inevitable sense of failure. Now because he had not taken up these opportunities he regarded himself as a failure and as having let down his wife and children.

John's EMIS was that 'I don't have what it takes, I am flawed'. The counsellor began challenging his EMIS by asking whether he would have regarded himself as flawed if he had not passed the examination at 11 and had gone to the local secondary modern school with his primary school friends, and he replied 'Probably not'. In the style of the television detective Columbo the counsellor expressed his confusion 'So, *but for* passing the exam you wouldn't have regarded yourself as flawed!'. The client replied 'I have often thought that before but now it seems crazy'. At this juncture the counsellor asked him how he had kept this prejudice against himself alive and he recalled that at grammar school he had derided a studious school mate only to find that he became a very famous playwright as an adult. The counsellor suggested that this was perhaps a somewhat arbitrary criterion and that he could equally have compared his subsequent progress to that of the child who had performed the poorest at primary school. John elaborated on the subsequent pathway of a child who lived in his road in primary school and went on to end up in prison. The counsellor then drew a line and put 'playwright' and 'prisoner' at opposite ends of the continuum and asked John to indicate where he would place himself. He indicated a position in the middle. (The use of continua in this way helps to challenge the black and white thinking of, for example, 'Either I am a success or I am a failure', so characteristic of depression). The counsellor summed up the situation by saying 'You are at least average in what you have achieved' but John quickly retorted 'I should have been near the high end'. At this the counsellor asked John to elaborate on why he wasn't further along the line. This produced a more explicit commitment on his part to the notion that it was his EMIS that had halted his progress along the continuum. The counsellor reiterated that 'But for the EMIS' his difficulties would not have developed.

The counsellor then constructed another continuum involving relationships with significant others. John was asked whether his relationship with his wife and children was better than most and he agreed that it was, which located him in one half of the continuum and then to place four other couples along this continuum. In fact he placed only one family more highly than his own. John was then asked which of the two dimensions 'achievement' and 'approval' he considered the more important and he replied 'At the end of the day it's the number of people around your grave that counts'.

In depression it is usually the case that clients implicitly rate themselves very negatively on either the 'achievement' or 'approval' continuum. The first step is to question their positioning on the salient negative continuum and if possible raise the significance of the more positive dimension. An often encountered problem when discussing EMISs is that the client agrees about the role of the EMIS but says 'That was the past, I can't change it so I am stuck'. The 'prejudice' model is particularly useful here, as it can be explained that when you have a prejudice derived from childhood you cannot stop the initial wave of 'dislike' but that you quickly check yourself and ensure that your actions are not consistent with the dislike nor do you make plans in terms of the dislike. It is important, however, to acknowledge the gut reaction, and not engage in emotional avoidance – a particular penchant of the personality disordered depressive. The gut reaction, after being acknowledged, is then treated with radical apathy, literally yawning and stretching at the prejudice, so the gut reaction itself is not treated as a moral matter. Similarly, the person with an EMIS has to deftly continue to step around it and not get agitated with its persistence. In time, like any prejudice deprived of action, it fades.

A particularly powerful way of challenging clients' excessive self-blame for mistakes that originated in childhood is to point out that the person they are blaming never existed. At the time the 'mistake' occurred there existed the child or adolescent in his or her naïvety, now there is the adult with the sophisticated knowledge of adults. The target of blame could justifiably have been the client as a child armed with the knowledge of the client as an adult, but such a person never existed. Clients are then asked to visualise their excessive self-blame being directed at a 'paper figure' of themselves with the wind of blame blowing right through the paper.

Key point

Clarify early maladaptive interpretations of self (EMISs) and early maladaptive expectations of others (EMEOs) by asking the client to describe concrete events surrounding his or her earliest distress and actions and goals at the time. Use the notion of 'Working to overcome a prejudice' to facilitate the modification of the EMISs. Continua can be very helpful in challenging client's dichotomous thinking. Explain that the target of excessive self-blame is often a person who never existed.

---

12   Tackle compensation for early maladaptive interpretations of self and others

On occasion clients cope with their EMISs and EMEOs by engaging in a strategy that is at the opposite extreme to that expected. For example, a very dependent client may exhibit a compulsive self-reliance, refusing reasonable offers of help or a client who believes him- or herself to be flawed or defective may, if placed in a group situation, attack other members for not sharing his or her values. When clients use compensation coping strategies they often increase interpersonal distance by either showing irritability themselves or eliciting irritability in others. Compensatory coping strategies are not the exclusive preserve of depressed clients but are often also exhibited by anxious clients who become exhausted. For example, Bart was a very successful senior manager. While he experienced intense anxiety at board level meetings, the consensus view in his organisation was that he was a man to be feared and 'ice-cold'. Bart himself defined his role as 'Picking holes in the ideas and plans of others' which he did with great ferocity. By his own admission he was a workaholic, and the imbalance in his life-style was a major factor in his brief affair with his secretary. His harsh exterior covered the inferiority he felt among colleagues who were mostly university educated.

It emerged that Bart's feelings of inferiority developed when he returned to school to resit his A levels. His EMIS was that he was a failure, and his EMEO of his contemporaries was that they would outshine him. Despite all his achievements in work in the 25 years since, the memory of walking down the long drive back to school for resits was still very vivid and upsetting to him. Bart was taught to use irritability as a cue that he may well be using a compensatory coping strategy and to consider that there may be a more efficient (and less emotionally draining) route to experiment with achieving his goal in a particular situation. Further, this alternative route would test out his EMEO that anything other than being 'ice-cold' would result in rejection thereby serving to maintain his EMIS.

The role of compensation seems particularly pronounced in clients who have a borderline personality disorder, whose behaviour often oscillates rapidly. At one moment their behaviour may be consistent with their EMIS and EMEO, say perhaps withdrawing from a group, and half an hour later they may be the centre of attention in the group, exhibiting outrageous behaviour and buying everyone drinks. This leads to a confused sense of identity and an emotional see-saw. For those close to them life is not predictable but the significant others often remain remarkably loyal because of the intermittent reinforcement they receive from the borderline personality disordered client. The compensatory behaviours are often so extreme, that they function as a 'fog' around the EMIS and EMEO. The borderline client appears to be in a permanent state of crisis as to preclude the counsellor focusing on the EMIS and EMEO. Possibly the commonest belief of the borderline client is 'If you really got to know me you would not like me', and these clients are often adept at superficial relationships but poor at intimate ones. The difficulty of the borderline client with intimacy unfortunately means counselling relationships are very difficult. The most likely scenario is that the counsellor will have a number of periods of brief contact with the client over a number of years perhaps modifying the compensatory strategy and more rarely changing the EMIS, resulting in a mellowing but with an associated mild to moderate depression.

> **Key point**
>
> Be aware that a client's coping strategy may be so extreme that it reflects central beliefs which are the exact opposite to those normally inferred by the behaviour.

13   Integrate basic cognitive-behavioural counselling with both a historical focus and relapse prevention strategies for depressed personality disordered clients

In this section a detailed case example is presented to illustrate how to blend traditional cognitive-behavioural counselling with the management of historical material and a focus on relapse prevention. The example chosen is based on a client seen by the first author and assessed, at that time, on DSM-III-R criteria (APA, 1987), as having both avoidant and dependent personality disorders. These two personality disorders are the most likely disorders across all the clusters to accompany depression and the following case describes the complexities of counselling a client with such co-morbidity.

Background

Catherine was suffering from a severe depression and was also highly anxious. Her immediate cause for concern was a restructuring at work in which she was moved to a new office with new procedures and personnel. Catherine claimed, however, that she had always been depressed but had simply covered it up well. She was a lone parent caring for her seven-year-old son Mark, and one of her current stressors was his natural father's turbulent behaviour with regard to access. Catherine's first marriage lasted less than twelve months and ended in divorce because of her husband's gay relationship. She had been brought up jointly by her maternal grandmother and mother, her own father dying when she was a young baby.

Psychopathology

Catherine was severely depressed with a score of 18 on the depression subscale of the Hospital Anxiety and Depression Scale (HAD: Snaith and Zigmond, 1983; range 0–21) and 16 on the anxiety subscale of the HAD (range 0–21), indicating moderate to severe anxiety. Her personality features were checked first against the DSM-III-R diagnostic criteria for dependent personality disorder, which are given in Table 13.1.

Catherine had always exhibited dependent behaviour and did so in a variety of contexts – such as, work, home, and so on. Thus the dependent and submissive behaviour was not just a feature of the current depressive episode, which indicated that the criteria shown in Table 13.1 for dependent personality disorder should be checked. In fact she met five of the criteria for dependent personality disorder:

Table 13.1 *Diagnostic criteria for dependent personality disorder*

A pervasive pattern of dependent and submissive behaviour, beginning by early adulthood and present in a variety of contexts, as indicated by at least five of the following:

1 is unable to make everyday decisions without an excessive amount of advice or reassurance from others
2 allows others to make most of his or her important decisions, for example, where to live, what job to take
3 agrees with people even when he or she believes they are wrong, due to fear of being rejected
4 has difficulty initiating projects or doing things on his or her own
5 volunteers to do things that are unpleasant or demeaning in order to get other people to like him or her
6 feels uncomfortable or helpless when alone, or goes to great lengths to avoid being alone
7 feels devastated or helpless when close relationships end
8 is frequently preoccupied with fears of being abandoned
9 is easily hurt by criticism or disapproval

Source: DSM-III-R

- 1 – for example, when shopping at a supermarket she would seek the advice of a companion as to whether a particular item was worth buying,
- 4 – for example, she had had the wallpaper and paint to decorate the small bedroom in her house for six months but had been unable to get started,
- 5 – for example, she had felt totally devastated both when her marriage ended and when her month-long relationship with Mark's father had ended,
- 8 – for example, had been terrified to express any criticism of her mother's and stepfather's handling of Mark, lest they abandon her, and
- 9 – for example, found even minor criticism so devastating that she compensated by working excessively hard in work to try and put herself beyond criticism.

In having five of the features of dependent personality disorder Catherine met the DSM-III-R criteria of the disorder. However, from a clinical point of view the number of features is less important than the way in which the criteria act as a useful description of her difficulties and thereby point towards particular interventions. Of course, the more features of a personality disorder a person has the more difficult he or she is to counsel, and the greater number of personality disorders from which an individual suffers the more difficult becomes the treatment.

Catherine's personality features were next checked against the DSM-III-R criteria for avoidant personality disorder which are summarised in Table 13.2.

Catherine reported she had always experienced social discomfort and been timid, and it was therefore important to test the appropriateness of an avoidant personality disorder description by utilising the criteria outlined in Table 13.2. Catherine met five of the seven criteria, thereby qualifying for the label avoidant personality disorder:

- 1 – for example, she would be very uncomfortable if, while shopping with a companion, the latter expressed disapproval over her enthusiasm for a particular purchase,
- 2 – for example, she had only one close friend,
- 5 – for example, in groups she would be extremely quiet for fear of saying the wrong thing,
- 6 – for example, she was excessively concerned that she blushed easily and that this was very visible to others,

Table 13.2 *Diagnostic criteria for avoidant personality disorder*

A pervasive pattern of social discomfort, fear of negative evaluation, and timidity, beginning by early adulthood and present in a variety of contexts, as indicated by at least four of the following:

1 is easily hurt by criticism or disapproval
2 has no close friends or confidant (or only one) other than first degree relatives
3 is unwilling to get involved with people unless certain of being liked
4 avoids social or occupational activities that involve significant interpersonal contact – for example, refuses a promotion that will increase social demands
5 is reticent in social situations because of a fear of saying something inappropriate or foolish, or of being unable to answer a question
6 fears being embarrassed by blushing, crying or showing signs of anxiety in front of other people
7 exaggerates potential difficulties, physical dangers or risks involved in doing something ordinary but outside of his or her usual routine – for example, may cancel social plans because he or she anticipates being exhausted by the effort of getting there

Source: DSM-III-R

- 7 – for example, became over-concerned that her employers wanted her to start earlier and finish earlier when in fact it only meant that she would be collecting her son from school instead of delivering him to school.

Conceptualisation

Catherine's earliest memories of distress went back to the time of entering junior school aged about seven. She believed she had to please both her mother and grandmother but that they were in competition for her affection. Whenever she made a choice between her 'mothers' she felt guilty. But for her Early Maladaptive Interpretation that 'I must please my "mothers" at all times in all circumstances' she would not have become depressed. As appropriate to her developmental stage she took her feelings of guilt as evidence that she must be guilty – a case of emotional reasoning. These guilt feelings together with the impossibility of living up to her self-imposed standards led her to a negative view of herself. This negative view of self was maintained in childhood by her belief that she was inferior to other children because she did not have the standard two parents. Her Early Maladaptive Expectation of Others, as it related to adults, was that there was no pleasing them but they were very competent and needed to get things done. The break-up of her marriage and of the relationship with Mark's father served to confirm the EMEO. The ways in which her mother and stepfather 'helped' her care for Mark served to heighten her sense of dependency. Her 'parents' critical comments of her, coupled with those of Mark's father, maintained her fear of people. Thus the possibility of being with new people in work had exacerbated her depression and the actuality of being with them had heightened her anxiety. Her maladaptive basic assumptions fell largely under Young's (1994) heading of 'other-directedness' described earlier in Section 6.

Treatment

Sessions 1 and 2

Sessions 1 and 2 were devoted to assessment using various psychological tests, distilling the above conceptualisation and giving a rationale for treatment. It is important to describe to the client the disorder by use of a metaphor that has direct therapeutic implications rather than in terms of, say, a biologically accurate explanation. That is, the metaphor used ought to be prescriptive rather than descriptive. In Catherine's case the counsellor suggested that 'It sounds like you have blown a fuse, everything has gone dead and you are on strike for better pay and conditions'. She was easily able to identify with this metaphor and a discussion was initiated as to what might constitute better 'pay and conditions' for her. This metaphor contains an implicit antidote to depression about depression in that it legitimises the depressive response – the inactivity – as a natural response to particularly disadvantageous circumstances.

During the second session the counsellor took the use of the metaphor further, suggesting that 'Maybe the "C" at the start of your name was for Cinderella not Catherine'. This led naturally to a discussion of how she could 'go to the ball' and the scheduling into her day of activities to give a sense of achievement and pleasure. Furthermore, it was going to be a question of her going to the ball rather than of the ball coming to her. For homework Catherine timetabled in potential uplifts to her week which included dancing to an aerobics video 3 times a week, and attempting some sketching at the weekend. It was stressed that at this stage it was a bonus if she actually enjoyed the uplifts, the goal was simply to overcome her inertia. Again metaphor was used – 'It's rather like pushing my heavy desk, once you get it moving it is not so bad but getting it moving in the first place is hard work!' To help her develop a sense of achievement it was suggested she break tasks down into small components and that after completion of each component she had a break and con- gratulated herself in some way for what she had accomplished so far.

Ideally the counsellor would have liked the individual sessions to have been complemented by group cognitive-behaviour therapy for depression but none was available locally at that time. The group modality is particularly appropriate for clients with avoidant personality disorder as it provides a powerful way in which EMEOs can be challenged. However, engagement of avoidant personality disorder clients is problematic precisely because they expect others to be critical and demeaning. This can be overcome by offering a package of initial individual sessions followed by group therapy then further individual sessions. In Catherine's case because she also had a dependent personality disorder there was a heightened risk that in individual therapy she would become dependent on the counsellor, a further reason why a group cognitive-behaviour therapy component to her treatment could have been particularly valuable.

Sessions 3 to 5

Sessions 3 to 5 began with reviews of Catherine's activity sched- uling. Her activities had, to her surprise, begun to lift her mood. This slight lifting of mood meant it was possible to begin working with her EMIS and EMEO. A start was made by asking how Mark, her son, would feel if she and her mother competed for his attention. Catherine thought he would be very confused, agitated and become fed up. She was then asked 'Should he blame himself for this stage of affairs?' and Catherine was adamant that he should not do so but possibly would do so. In this way she was helped to appreciate how she herself had begun to become depressed and that she was not blameworthy.

Session 6

Session 6 was something of a setback as Catherine was so pre- occupied with the way in which Mark's father had, once again, let Mark down. As a result, the counsellor had to give up the attempt to negotiate a shared agenda for the session. Apparently Mark's father had promised to collect him at 9 a.m. on the

Table 13.3   *Problem solving*

1 Define the problem in terms as specific and concrete as possible.
2 Write down as many possible solutions to the problem as possible, going for quantity of solutions rather than quality.
3 Go through the advantages and disadvantages of each solution both in the short term and in the long term.
4 Choose a solution.
5 Plan the steps necessary to implement the chosen solution.
6 Review the solution in the light of experience, if necessary recycling to step 2 and trying another solution.

Saturday to take him fishing for the day and he had telephoned at 4 p.m., obviously drunk, to say he could not make it. Unfortunately, Mark blamed his mother for his father not turning up 'Because you always shout at him when he comes' and she was exhausted having to endure his tantrums for the whole weekend. After almost 30 minutes of Catherine's tirade about Mark's father, the counsellor asked whether it actually helped to go on about how awful the situation was, as she had been having these tirades for years. This tendency to repeatedly 'awfulise' is quite common in depression and can lead to a deficit in the first stage of problem solving, that of problem orientation such that the person does not properly 'lock onto' problems. At an intellectual level Catherine was quite able to solve a given problem with 'pen and paper' as it were, indeed she was struck by how easily she could solve her one friend Mary's problems but could not solve her own. Again the counsellor used a metaphor to explain problem orientation – 'It is as if you do not actually place the spanner over the nut in the first place, though you obviously have the strength to turn it'. (A useful procedure with clients who persistently awfulise and will not problem orientate is to do a role reversal, but this should only be attempted when some rapport is established.)

The counsellor then introduced the problem solving pro forma shown in Table 13.3 to tackle the difficulties about Mark's father, in this way creating space to again work with the EMIS and EMEO at the following sessions by lifting Catherine's mood. As the counsellor began explaining the pro forma Catherine kept saying 'I will have to do something, it's awful' rather than taking in the details of the problem solving process, the need for specificity, and so on. She was thus peripherally rather than centrally processing what the counsellor was saying. The counsellor halted the explanation of the pro forma and asked 'For how long have you thought that it's awful and that you must do something about it?' and she replied that it had been a problem for over a year. The counsellor's next question was whether there had been any value in the past year, or indeed now, in 'Just going on about it'. Rather sheepishly she replied that it did not serve any purpose.

Catherine was exhibiting a problem common to many depressives in that they do not problem orient. Following the Flemming and Pretzer (1990) guidelines on the importance of using the data of transactions with the counsellor to effect change in clients with a personality disorder, the counsellor pointed out how her 'awfulising' was getting in the way of her picking up the problem solving procedure. She had little difficulty with steps one to three of the problem solving process, though she was somewhat surprised when the counsellor suggested that how she handled the situation over the past year should be listed as a theoretical option, making the point that doing nothing was itself a choice and she had to take responsibility if she chose to exercise it.

When Catherine came to Step 4, choosing a solution, her dependent personality disorder was much in evidence. She began asking the counsellor 'But what do you think I should do?' This again was an opportunity to use 'hot' material to better make a therapeutic point so the counsellor replied with a question 'But does it work for you asking other people what you should do and following through on that?' and Catherine agreed that her approach had only meant she had ended up having to seek professional help. The counsellor thought it also important to disavow Catherine of two important beliefs that nurtured her deficit in independent decision making. The first was that other people 'just knew' what should be done. Again the counsellor used metaphor to make the point 'No one has a crystal ball, everyone is just making informed guesses'. A deficit in independent decision making is the hallmark of clients with dependent personality disorder and a major counselling target. The second belief was that the decision chosen 'Had to be the right one'. This concern to 'get it right' had, in Catherine's case and in the case of many depressives, led to procrastination and then depression about the indecisiveness. Within the above problem solving framework it was explained that most options chosen are at best partial solutions and it would be necessary to adapt or try other solutions subsequently, returning to the menu of options at Step 2.

In the past Catherine had been inhibited because she believed that if any solution did not work out fully then she was necessarily to blame. She automatically personalised difficulties, rather than seeing hassles as an integral part of life which could be dealt with, though with varying degrees of skill. Catherine eventually decided on leaving Mark each Sunday afternoon at his paternal grandparents with whom he had a good relationship, and they would discreetly endeavour to contact their son and see if he was going to visit.

Session 7

At the start of this session Catherine was reassessed and found to be moderately as opposed to severely depressed. Her previous week's homework was reviewed and she had now arranged for Mark to visit his paternal grandparents. Catherine had been tempted however to cancel the arrangement because, she said, the grandparents had not been entirely happy about it. When pressed further it emerged that they had not actually expressed any unwillingness about making the arrangement, they were simply not enthusiastic about it. This highlighted her basic assumption that she should never inconvenience or irritate anyone. Much of the earlier part of the session was devoted to a discussion about the impossibility of living without inconveniencing or irritating someone. Catherine conceded that she accepted other people's right to inconvenience her and that therefore she had a right to inconvenience others. The notion of balancing one's needs against those of others was introduced as the model of assertive behaviour. For homework it was decided that Catherine would tackle this oversensitivity to the needs of others by challenging her mother and stepfather's discriminatory handling of Mark compared with his cousin. This also involved a testing out of her basic assumption that she would ultimately end up disconnected from them and rejected. Part of Catherine's depression arose because she believed herself to be disconnected from others and wanted to overcome this isolation. However she was in a dilemma because her EMEO was that others would be critical and demeaning. This dilemma is usually at the heart of the difficulties of clients who are depressed with a co-morbid avoidant personality disorder. For homework it was agreed that she would begin testing out this belief that her 'audience' in life was uniformly and wholly negative by putting her name down to attend the forthcoming Christmas night out at work and at the next counselling session her concerns about 'surviving' this experience would be addressed.

Session 8

This session was devoted to Catherine's surviving social encounters. She was very concerned that she did not know what to say in social encounters and that she led such a boring life that nobody would be interested. The counsellor noted that Catherine in fact had no particular social skill deficits: she made eye contact appropriately, smiled and interacted quite satisfactorily. (Had there been deficits in these areas, they would have needed to be addressed: see Scott, 1989.) Her social difficulties were, rather, a product of unreasonable expectations – that there should never be any silences, that she should always have something stimulating to say – and her mistaken belief that conversation was wholly about content as opposed to a vehicle for conveying interest in or appreciation of another person. It was agreed that the main task therefore was to overcome her avoidance of social encounters. She agreed to go to the canteen at work for lunch rather than eat sandwiches at her desk in her office, and to investigate the possibilities of going to a night school class.

Sessions 9 to 15

These sessions were scheduled every two weeks to help prevent dependence on the counsellor. During these sessions the prime focus was on the automatic thoughts that recurred on Catherine's Managing Distress form – 'I'm not special to anyone' and 'There is no one there for me when I need them'. These thought patterns were triggered by the placing of herself in increasingly more social situations such as lunching with colleagues and hearing of their relationships. Indeed the previous avoidance of these situations could be construed as emotional avoidance – that is, avoiding the painful affect these situations might trigger.

The counsellor first sought to clarify the meaning of 'I'm not special to anyone' and in so doing Catherine agreed that she was special to Mark, somewhat less so to her brother, and of much less significance to her mother. This again was a challenge to Catherine's tendency to dichotomous thinking – 'I'm either special or not special'. It transpired that what Catherine was particularly grieving over was the absence of an exclusive close intimate relationship and the hopelessness of initiating one. Once again the problem solving pro forma was used and Catherine decided that she would join Gingerbread, a self-help group for single parent families, because that was a non-threatening context in which she might meet a partner while at the same time catering for the constraints of being a single parent. This also opened up the possibility of developing confiding relationships. By way of preparation the counsellor role-played with Catherine attending a Gingerbread meeting with Mark. The counsellor placed a special emphasis on the need to tolerate the discomfort of first meetings and not to prematurely escape. Specifically it was agreed that Catherine would challenge any 'I can't stand it' thoughts with 'The discomfort passes, I am not going to curl up and die, it is short-term pain for long-term gain'. This last thought was put on a flashcard for a homework in which she was to look at it as often as practical when she sat down or had a drink.

Session 16

By session 16 Catherine was no longer depressed and had made some friends at the self-help group. The counsellor's concerns at this stage were that she should attribute her improvement to specific changes in thinking and behaviour and be aware of likely precipitants of relapse and of the appropriate coping strategies. Catherine was first asked by the counsellor what she had found most helpful in the sessions. She replied that it was the ability to separate out the past from the present, specifically the 'fusion technique' that the counsellor taught. In the fusion technique, when the client has a strong emotional reaction to a situation or thought the client is asked to join (fuse) his or her hands together and then consider whether they ought to be drawn apart with one hand representing aspects of the past and the other aspects of the present, and the latter – 'present' – hand dealt with on its own, symbolically clenched and relaxed.

The other major turning point in counselling came from viewing her inactivity and 'drifting' at the start of therapy as a choice she had made and agreeing that she could choose better. The counsellor suggested that she should make her own 'first aid' book about what she had learnt to be used in the event of an emergency. The counsellor explained that if she was ever depressed, something written in her own words as an aid to coping with relapse was likely to have more immediate impact than, say, trying to use or recall the Managing Distress Form. However, the counsellor noticed that Catherine seemed uncomfortable and fidgety with this discussion. (This highlights the importance, particularly with personality disordered clients, of paying as much attention to non-verbal communications as to verbal ones.) The counsellor asked her why she had become suddenly 'edgy'. She replied that she did not want to think about relapse, and that she had spent too much of her life being negative. At this the counsellor asked how she was going to feel if she had a relapse and she answered that she would be 'Devastated'. The counsellor explained that overcoming depression was rather like a smoker giving up cigarettes. Most people successfully manage to give up cigarettes at the fourth or fifth attempt and so long as they learn from their earlier slips success is assured. The important strategy is to stop any slips becoming full-blown relapses by the implementation of specific strategies. For depression, it was explained that it was necessary to clarify and overlearn the relapse prevention strategies at an opportune time when she was asymptomatic so that they were still accessible amidst the disorientation that a slip brings.

Attention was then focused on the particular scenarios that might usher in a slip. Catherine developed a list that included any breakdown of the new relationships she was forming and Mark's paternal grandparents pulling out of the access arrangements. It was suggested that in her first aid book she might write detailed coping strategies for these scenarios. Catherine's initial reluctance to discuss relapse prevention strategies showed how pervasive her cognitive avoidance was even when free of depressive symptoms, and this constituted an ongoing vulnerability factor. It is therefore particularly important to schedule in booster sessions for clients with a personality disorder as well as providing an emergency helpline.

Booster session 1

The first booster session took place six weeks later at which Catherine reported no further symptoms of depression. She was becoming more outgoing and had developed a particular friendship with a man called John at Gingerbread. As with all counselling sessions at the start of the session the counsellor had negotiated with the client her agenda for the session. The counsellor was encouraged that Catherine showed no resistance to reviewing relapse prevention strategies and these were made the main focus of the session.

Booster session 2

The second booster session took place three months after the first. By this session Catherine had had a relapse, she was highly anxious and moderately depressed. The major difficulty on which she wished to focus in the session was her relationship with John. She was very undecided on whether to end the relationship or not and wanted advice on what to do. In the discussion that followed her originally diagnosed dependent personality disorder was much in evidence. First the counsellor encouraged her to juxtapose the good and bad things about the relationship, to help her see that reality was complex and that given such complexity no one, including the counsellor, could be sure what a 'right' decision would be. Catherine then remembered from earlier sessions that she had come to believe that she was as likely to be right about something as anyone else. The counsellor suggested that perhaps she had been reverting to being the little girl again, imagining others knew better and she appreciated that this was the case. It seemed also that Catherine was engaged in dichotomous thinking: either the relationship was 'Superb' (as it had been in the first few weeks) or it was 'The pits' and the counsellor put both these points at either end of a continuum and then suggested that there was a mid-way position of being 'just reasonably content' (JRC).

The counsellor then asked her to comment on whether or not she might be around this middle point and Catherine agreed that for probably most of her time with John the relationship had moved either side of the JRC point. In passing she mentioned 'Sometimes John is just like Mark's father'. This alerted the counsellor that the predominance of anxiety rather than depression symptoms at present might be because now that the relationship had developed she had a heightened fear of rejection and abandonment, the fear of rejection resonating with the originally diagnosed avoidant personality disorder. It was agreed that Catherine would practise the 'fusion technique' to help separate what was actually going on at present in the relationship with John from the fears and beliefs of the little girl.

Booster session 3

The third booster session was arranged just six weeks after the second in view of Catherine's deterioration. The counsellor however resisted making any earlier appointment because of Catherine's dependent personality features. By this session Catherine had regained the ground she had lost at the previous session. The counsellor asked her how she had made the recovery and she said that she had found it very helpful to constantly remind herself that 'Everything isn't a matter of life and death' (an antidote to dichotomous thinking). A final booster session was arranged for three months hence, and it was agreed that if she was free of symptoms then subsequent contact would be left open.

Booster session 4

Catherine was still symptom free by this session and it was agreed not to schedule a further session but that she could make contact if she really needed to.

The above case example illustrates that when a depressed client has a personality disorder (avoidant and dependent personality disorders being the most common) any relapse is almost always associated with the personality disorder features. Further, an initial response to counselling is also more difficult to achieve in depressed clients with co-morbid personality disorder. The contact arrangement for depressed clients with co-morbid personality disorder reflects a belief that currently these clients are best regarded as suffering from a chronic condition, the psychological equivalents of diabetics for whom periodic booster sessions are going to be necessary but who can be enabled to function well for most of the time. By contrast, depressed clients without a personality disorder can be thought of as suffering from an acute condition for whom 'cure' is possible. The meaningfulness of these distinctions will only be determined when the requisite controlled trials of depressed clients with and without co-morbid personality disorders are conducted.

Key point

Depressed clients with a personality disorder may well be more the psychological equivalent of a diabetic for whom life-long periodic boosters are the most likely scenario. Nevertheless, particularly if their co-morbidity is an 'anxious' personality disorder, they can be enabled to function most of the time. As the personality disordered client's difficulties are largely interpersonal, a group intervention should be a part of the intervention.

III Anxiety Disorders

14 Explain to the client that generalised anxiety disorder is an erroneous attempt to justify tension

Generalised anxiety disorder (GAD) only became a recognised and reliable diagnostic category with the publication of the revised third edition of the Diagnostic and Statistical Manual of Mental Disorders (DSM-III-R, American Psychiatric Association, 1987) and so studies attesting to the efficacy of interventions for GAD are much fewer than for, say, depression. Part of the hesitancy in defining it as a disorder has been that many individuals report the disorder as being life-long, with as many as 80 per cent not being able to recall its emergence (Rapee, 1991). This has led to the suggestion that GAD should more properly be described as an 'anxious personality disorder' but in fact in DSM-IV it has been retained as an emotional disorder with the diagnostic criteria shown in Table 14.1.

Criterion A in DSM-IV specifies that the worry must be excessive – that is, the intensity, duration and frequency of the worry is out of proportion to the likelihood or impact of the feared event. Further, that the worry is not just a response to transient events but has been an important feature of the previous six months. Criterion B requires that the individual perceives the worry as difficult to control. Again in Criterion C there is a requirement that the symptoms experienced from the list have to have been a prominent feature of the past six months. Criterion D makes clear that the anxiety or worry must not be about specific other Axis 1 concerns, for example, having a panic attack (as in Panic Disorder), being embarrassed in public (as in Social Phobia), being contaminated (as in Obsessive-Compulsive Disorder) and is not part of post-traumatic stress disorder. This particular requirement for GAD suggests that this disorder is perhaps the basic anxiety disorder and that later it may be transformed into another disorder when the content of the apprehensive expectation becomes more specific, such as panic attacks.

Table 14.1   *Diagnostic criteria for generalised anxiety disorder*

A Excessive anxiety and worry (apprehensive expectation) about a number of events or activities (such as work or school performance), occurring more days than not, for at least six months.

B The person finds it difficult to control the worry.

C The anxiety and worry are associated with at least three of the following six symptoms (with at least some symptoms present for more days than not for the past six months):

   1 restlessness or feeling keyed up or on edge
   2 being easily fatigued
   3 difficulty in concentrating or mind going blank
   4 irritability
   5 muscle tension
   6 sleep disturbance (difficulty in falling or staying asleep, or restless unsatisfying sleep).

D The focus of the anxiety and worry is not confined to features of an Axis 1 disorder.

E The anxiety, worry, or physical symptoms significantly interfere with the person's normal routine or usual activities, or there is marked distress.

F Not due to the direct effect of a substance or a general medical condition and does not occur exclusively during a Mood Disorder, Psychotic Disorder, or a Pervasive Developmental Disorder.

Source: DSM-IV

GAD clients can often be distinguished from other anxious clients by their answer to the question, 'Do you worry excessively about minor matters?' A client replying 'No' to this question is extremely unlikely to be suffering from GAD. However, a positive response to the question does not of itself decide which disorder they are suffering from.

At present there are no prospective studies of the development of GAD nor even any strong retrospective studies. One retrospective study found that students who qualified for GAD on the basis of a questionnaire measure (known to have a 20 per cent false-positive rate compared with a structured interview) were more likely than controls to describe their mothers as rejecting and having an enmeshed relationship (Roemer et al., 1991): they also had more angry and oscillating feelings towards their mothers. The validity of these retrospective perceptions of childhood and their specific relation to personality, however, is not known. This does suggest though that historical enquiries with GAD clients may be important to distil the way in which their apprehensive expectations developed. The enquiry is somewhat more difficult than with depressed clients in that it is less likely for there to be discrete traumatic events that stand out – that is, it is not a particular episodic memory being operative but rather a more general semantic memory. Clinical experience suggests that the mother of the GAD client often responded to hassles as catastrophes and this has led to the development of apprehensive expectation in the client. This state of anxious apprehension is associated with a state of high negative affect and chronic overarousal, a sense of uncontrollability and an attentional focus on threat related stimuli (for example, high self-focused attention or self-preoccupation and hypervigilance). The anxiety is represented at a physiological level by the types of symptoms described in Criterion C in Table 14.1 and these are the symptoms the adult client with GAD readily volunteers.

Traditionally, cognitive-behaviour therapy has emphasised the role cognitions play in influencing affect but in fact the cognitive-behavioural model described in the Introduction, Figure I.1, shows the reciprocity between cognitions, physiology and affect. It is suggested that in GAD the individual attempts to explain physiological and emotional symptoms in terms of threats from the environment. It is a case of affect capturing cognitions – namely, of the GAD sufferer developing what Wessler (1993) has termed 'justifying cognitions'. The justifying cognition is negatively reinforcing in that it gives individuals some sense of relief by appearing to explain why they are the way they are. Because the justifying cognition is a means to an end rather than an end in itself it is, in the language of the Elaboration Likelihood Model of Persuasion (Petty and Cacioppo, 1986; Stoltenberg et al., 1989), peripherally rather than centrally processed. The individual does not spend long enough elaborating on the justifying cognition to see that the threat element it contains is largely unfounded. If subsequently the particular justifying cognition is shown to be without validity, because it was only peripherally processed in the first place, it is easily dismissed with some rule of thumb such as 'I was lucky there, it didn't turn out so bad' and the focus quickly moves to some other justifying cognition. Not surprisingly the individual eventually complains of not being able to control the worry.

A client can attempt a permanent justification for his or her state of anxious apprehension by adopting a philosophy of 'constructive pessimism', and this leads to a mild depression often being associated with the GAD. The rationale for constructive pessimism is that the individual is better prepared for life and therefore more able to cope. What this means in fact is that when things go better than expected the individual has in the process become so highly anxious that he or she is unable to savour the good fortune and so quickly focuses on another calamity to justify the anxious emotional state. By the time clients come for counselling they are already becoming aware that the contents of their concerns are without substance and their focus is on worry about their mental life, that is, their major problem is now meta-worry.

Key point

Conceptualise generalised anxiety disorder as an attempt to justify distressing physiological symptoms utilising threats from the environment. When one threat is found to be without foundation it makes little difference to the client – the focus turns to another threat. The degree of threat in any particular situation is characteristically exaggerated.

---

15 Target tension with generalised anxiety disordered clients

The client's tension can be targeted with relaxation training. This begins with discrimination training, noting the differences between tension and relaxation. The body is first compartmenta-lised into the following 16 muscle groups:

1 right hand and lower arm
2 left hand and lower arm
3 right upper arm
4 left upper arm
5 right lower leg and foot
6 left lower leg and foot
7 thighs
8 abdomen
9 chest and breathing
10 shoulders
11 lower neck
12 back of neck

13 lips
14 eyes
15 lower forehead
16 upper forehead

Each of the 16 muscle groups is noted by individually tensing them in the order above. After a 'right–left' sequence, both limbs are tensed together. The next stage is to:

1 tense the muscle groups for 5 to 10 seconds;
2 attend to the sensation of tension in that muscle group and area of the body;
3 relax the muscle for 10 to 15 seconds; and
4 notice the difference between tension and relaxation.

Ideally the client should practise this progressive relaxation for 15–20 minutes, twice a day.

Initially the counsellor should take the client through this procedure to check there are no difficulties with its implementation. It is useful to audio-tape the counsellor's instructions and this can be taken away by the client to guide the client through the exercise. A minority of clients experience relaxation-induced anxiety, fearing either losing control or the floating sensation. In some instances clients will as a consequence refuse to partake in the procedures. However, they often seem to be the clients who tend to try and overcontrol things in their life and who, as a consequence of trying to ward off imagined catastrophes, often exhaust themselves. It is helpful with this subgroup to suggest that sometimes one is more in control of a situation by 'Having a light touch on the steering wheel' than by gripping it firmly and that they might test out their belief that there will be dire consequences by relaxing, practising progressive relaxation on a daily basis. Thus, though within the cognitive model entry has been made through the physiological port a simultaneous advance through the cognitive port may be necessary. (Further it may be necessary to tackle the exhaustion of the generalised anxiety disorder client simultaneously through the behavioural port with time management techniques.) To aid the transition to a more normal setting the client should be seated in a comfortable chair in the counsellor's office. The progressive relaxation is introduced at the start of counselling generalised anxiety disorder clients and typically lasts for two weeks.

The second stage of relaxation training is 'release only'. The aim of this stage is to reduce the time it takes to relax by omitting tension. The release-only exercise is conducted by the client for five to seven minutes twice a day. Typical instructions given by the counsellor (Ost, 1987: 409) are as follows:

> Breathe with calm, regular breaths and feel yourself relaxing more and more with every breath . . . just let go . . . relax your forehead . . . eyebrows . . . eyelids . . . jaws . . . tongue and throat . . . your entire face . . . relax your neck . . . shoulders . . . arms . . . and all the way down to your finger-tips . . . continue to breathe calmly and regularly with your stomach . . . let the feeling of relaxation spread to your stomach . . . waist and back . . . relax the lower part of your body, your bottom . . . thighs . . . knees . . . calves . . . feet . . . and all the way down to the tip of your toes . . . breathe calmly and regularly and feel how you relax more and more with each breath . . . take a deep breath and hold it for a couple of seconds . . . and let the air out slowly . . . slowly . . . notice how you relax more and more.

If a particular muscle group is difficult to relax, clients are asked to tense it briefly and then release it again. Clients are asked to practise release-only relaxation twice a day for one or two weeks.

The third stage of relaxation training is cue-controlled relaxation, in which the aim is to achieve a state of relaxation in two to three minutes. In the counselling session the counsellor first asks the client to relax using release-only relaxation, then just before an inhalation the counsellor says 'Inhale' and just before an exhalation, the counsellor says 'Relax'. This sequence is repeated five times and then the client is instructed to continue the sequence silently. After a further minute, the counsellor once again says 'Inhale . . . relax' several times, then the client again continues solo for several minutes. Cue-controlled relaxation is practised twice a day for one or two weeks before moving on to the next stage.

The fourth stage of relaxation training is differential relaxation and its purpose is to learn how to relax while engaged in everyday activities in roughly 60–90 seconds. First the client is told to use cue-controlled relaxation to relax, then to move one muscle group while simultaneously relaxing all other groups. Each muscle group is activated in turn while relaxing all other groups. The body is scanned by the client to identify any muscle group not being relaxed. Initially the client is taught differential relaxation in an armchair and practises the strategy in that context for a week or two before practising it when standing or walking.

The fifth stage of relaxation training is rapid relaxation in which cues are placed in the environment – for example, a coloured mark on the telephone as a signal to relax. The aim is to relax 15–20 times a day in non-stressful situations. When relaxing the client is instructed to first take one to three deep breaths, slowly exhaling after each breath and to think 'Relax' before each exhalation. Simultaneously the client is asked to scan the body for tension and try to relax as much as possible in the situation. The aim of this stage is to become able to relax in 20–30 seconds.

The final stage of relaxation training is application training in which the client exposes him- or herself for 10–15 minutes at a time to the situations which are anxiety evoking and practises the relaxation response. Exposure should be to a wide range of anxiety evoking situations, with frequent daily practice. The client is inoculated against failure experiences by being told that the relaxation response is an acquired art taking much practice and there are inevitable slips.

The importance of relaxation training (or for that matter medication) is that it helps remove the physiological cue to hunt for a justifying cognition. The generalised anxiety disordered client's state of apprehensive expectation represents the cognitive and emotional correlate of physiological tension and is targeted in the next section.

Key point

A state of relaxation is incompatible with the excessive worry over minor matters that characterises generalised anxiety disorder. In relaxation training, practice moves from tensing and relaxing each muscle group in turn while away from the stressful situation, to eventually using cues such as 'Inhale . . . relax' when under stress. Some clients can initially become more distressed by relaxation training because they fear a loss of control if they relax.

---

16 Target apprehensive expectation with generalised anxiety disordered clients

In generalised anxiety disorder there is a mismatch between a client's expectations and his or her experiences. It is important to highlight this gap between expectations and what is actually experienced. This can be done quite simply by asking the client to rate on a scale from 1 to 10 a prediction as to how awful something is going to be and then to make a rating after the event. The two numbers used in the ratings, say 8 and 6, can be used subsequently as a shorthand reminder when the client becomes anxious anticipating that forthcoming events will be pretty awful (a rating of 8) when in fact they turn out to be not that bad (a rating of 6).

The expectations of generalised anxiety disordered clients have a catastrophic flavour, their vividness serving to ensure that the data of their experiences is only peripherally processed. To take an example Stanley had been unjustly reprimanded by his boss following a complaint about him by a member of the public. Stanley had worked for his employer for ten years with no complaints, but after his reprimand he lived in fear of his telephone ringing lest it was his boss with another reprimand, and he went off work sick. In counselling he became aware that he felt worse before going into work than when he was at work – namely, there was a mismatch between expectation and experience. The counsellor first asked Stanley to calculate the chances of a member of the public making a complaint (a) and of his boss reprimanding him following a complaint (b) and then went on to explain that the odds for the worst case scenario were (a) multiplied by (b). Generalised anxiety disorder clients have a preference for persistently mentally rehearsing 'worst case' scenarios and it is therefore important to help them appreciate that the chances of this coming to pass are indeed remote. Having calculated the statistical odds it is necessary to ground them in some aspect of experience, for example the odds might be likened to the chances of them having a traffic accident or even more remotely a fatal accident. The analogous risks carry the implicit

Table 16.1 *Thought record*

1 *Trigger* – what happened/the nature of the troublesome thoughts
2 *Emotion* – what you felt
3 *Automatic thought* – what it sounds 'As if' you said to yourself about the trigger
4 *Rational response* – the most realistic interpretation of the situation

message that they are doing nothing new in taking risks, indeed living is impossible without risks, but they are calculated risks and they are most likely to be safe.

Teaching the GAD client to tolerate the discomfort caused by taking calculated risks is another important strategy. If the client continues to seek and is given reassurance every time risk is involved it serves in the long term to feed the client's apprehensive expectation even though in the short term it produces a sense of relief. For example, if one of a client's worries is about someone close to him or her having a traffic accident, the client should be discouraged from telephoning a recent visitor to his or her home to check that the visitor arrived at the destination safely.

As an aid to focusing on the data of their experience clients should be encouraged to complete the Thought Record, given in Table 16.1, when they become unduly apprehensive.

The first step in completing the Thought Record is to identify the trigger. This may be an actual situation such as being called to a meeting with the boss, or it may be a troublesome thought such as 'I am just not up to this course'. The second step identifies the emotion associated with the trigger. In the third step the mental response to the trigger is identified. This might be 'I will probably get told off for something by the boss' or 'I am not up to this course, I am not up to anything, never have been'. The fourth step involves a critical appraisal of the automatic thought, asking whether the data of the person's experience supports his or her interpretation, such as 'I have never been put down by this boss before, why should I expect it now?' In some instances a person's negative inference about a situation may seem highly likely. In these circumstances it is often possible to challenge the client's evaluation of the trigger by asking the client to explore it on a 'So what if . . . ' basis and thereby challenge the catastrophic nature of his or her thoughts.

To help GAD clients 'de-catastrophise' it is useful for them to locate the everyday hassles they experience along a mountain–molehill continuum as shown in Figure 16.1.

At the start of a counselling session the counsellor asked the

Figure 16.1   *Mountain–molehill continuum*

client, Fiona, how she had been since the last counselling session. As always she replied with a tale of woe. This week her catastrophes included being unable to switch on her gas fire (an alternative source of heat was available), and having to wait three days for the weather to become suitable for her husband to repair a leak from the gutter into their house. The counsellor first asked the client to recall her worst event in recent years and this was labelled the mountain. Then she was asked to think of something that didn't really matter though she would prefer it had not happened, and this was the molehill. The next step was to have her locate the two hassles since the last session along the line and she in fact placed both of them on the molehill side of the continuum but not as trivial as the molehill itself. For homework she was asked to shout 'Stop!' to herself whenever a hassle occurred, visualise a set of traffic lights on red, then as the lights changed to amber she was to locate the hassle along the continuum. Finally when the lights went to green she was to go about her business telling herself 'Not to make mountains out of molehills'.

Some of the thoughts of generalised anxiety disordered clients can verge on an obsession and clinical experience suggests that the Thought Record has little lasting impact on these. Probably the most common themes are social concerns about possible embarrassment, or health concerns. It is useful to have these clients construct a 'reality audio-tape' which describes the most probable sequence of events, that is the events that are statistically most likely.

For example Jane was preoccupied with the idea that her two-year-old child would never survive to adulthood but could well meet with a horrific death beforehand. She was a nurse and had herself witnessed many child deaths. To prepare for the making of the 'reality tape' Jane was asked to close her eyes and describe taking her son to school on his first day, and then to describe how she might take him to cubs and which other children might be going as well, then to her reactions to his first girlfriend and so on right to the birth of her first grandchild. The rationale for doing this is that people become more committed to that which they verbalise and this exercise 'primed the pump' for her making the reality tape. Jane was asked to play the reality tape at a fixed time for 20 minutes each day and was instructed that when thoughts of an accident came to mind at other times she was calmly to say to herself 'The reality of the matter is on tape; I can and will listen to that later'. At the next counselling session Jane complained that the tone of her voice on the tape was not convincing and the counsellor explained that this was highly likely and that 'reality' could only percolate through to a 'gut' level and the evidence that it was beginning to do so was in an already reduced frequency of the catastrophic thought.

Key point

A major focus with GAD clients is to alter their expectations so that they more closely match their experience. This may be achieved through the use of 'reality audio-tapes' and/or Thought Records. The tendency of GAD clients to catastrophise may be tackled using the 'mountain–molehill' continuum.

---

17 Target meta-worry with generalised anxiety disordered clients

For some GAD clients it is not specific worries that are a particular cause for concern but rather worrying about worry and experiencing thoughts as uncontrollable and involuntary. This is termed meta-worry. Wells (1994) has commented that meta-worry appears to reflect both a negative appraisal of the significance of a thought and also difficulties with thought regulation. The meta-worry subscale of his Anxious Thoughts Inventory contains beliefs such as 'I think that I am missing out on things in life because I worry too much', 'Unpleasant thoughts enter my mind against my will' and 'I worry that I cannot control my thoughts as well as I would like to'.

The 'worry-time' technique addresses the thought regulation dimension of meta-worry by suggesting to a client that when a repetitive worry presents which is inappropriate for the task in hand the client instructs him- or herself to postpone addressing it to a specific time, to be sorted out properly in a worry half-hour. The rationale given is that 30 minutes' worry a day is more than enough for anyone! It should be noted that this is not encouraging the client towards cognitive avoidance but a way for the client to tackle the problematic thoughts at a more appropriate time.

GAD clients practise cognitive avoidance by telling themselves not to think about what is worrying them. This has the opposite effect to that intended. The shortcomings of the client's traditional approach can be highlighted by the counsellor saying 'If I asked you not to think about pink elephants (pause) then it makes you think about them more'. The counsellor should then go on to explain that injunctions from friends and family to 'Don't worry about it' generally have the opposite effect. Typically clients are relieved that their unexpressed wish that others would stop saying 'Don't worry' is legitimised. Often they have felt inhibited from saying anything because of the well-meaning intent of others.

It is useful for clients to use pen and paper in their worry half hour as this creates a degree of objectivity about their worries. Clients may also use the Thought Record during this time. It is important to stress that the worry-time technique is much simpler to comprehend than to implement and that initially its effects may be marginal but that with continued practise they become more pronounced. The difficulty is that the client has to keep a matter-of-fact stance to thoughts which will, at least to begin with, probably regularly intrude.

The worry-time technique mainly addresses the thought regulation aspect of meta-worry and further strategies are required to tackle the significance of the thoughts. While many GAD clients are aware that their current main concern could easily be dislodged and seem in retrospect as 'Much ado about nothing', nevertheless at the time a particular worry is at its height it is very disturbing. Often clients are disturbed that a particular thought could well lead to their acting upon it. It is important with these clients to make the distinction between the presence of a thought and plans for implementation of a thought and that it is the latter that leads to action. The persistent presence of a thought does not usher in action, rather the latter is preceded by a specific plan. When a disturbing thought is persistent much of a client's exhaustion arises from trying to battle against the thought, to neutralise it.

Rather than neutralise the thought by trying to argue against or avoid it, the client should be encouraged to develop a 'radical apathy' about the thought. For example, Daniel became alarmed at the recurrent thought 'I could kill all my family'. This distressed him greatly as he had a good relationship with his wife and two children. He was first taught that everybody gets inappropriate thoughts and that he was only unusual in declaring his and attaching a particular significance to it. For homework Daniel was asked to regularly remind himself that 'Thoughts do not lead to action, only specific plans do' and that when the thoughts that he could kill his family came to mind he was to, literally, stretch and yawn at the thought and say 'What a bore'. After three weeks' practice this thought was rendered insignificant.

The content of the significant disturbing thought can itself be meta-cognitive. For example, Denise would be waking up in the morning or be at a social function and would begin thinking 'But will I ever get better, will I ever really be happy?' Indeed in a counselling session she would suddenly shift the discussion away from the topic under focus to these meta-cognitive concerns. The counsellor found it useful to label these concerns as 'TIC' – task interfering cognitions – as opposed to 'TOC' – task oriented concerns. Further she was to remind herself to switch from the former to the latter by saying 'TIC-TOC' and as the mnemonic suggests this would need to be a regular rhythm for her. It was agreed that her TOCs would focus on her plans and the likely sequence of events for the next three hours.

Key point

'Worry about worry' – meta-worry – often needs tackling with GAD clients. Meta-worry may be addressed by thought regulation strategies such as worry time and challenging the significance of the worry. It is important to stress that thoughts are not actions.

---

18   Teach panic disorder and agoraphobic clients to challenge catastrophic misinterpretations of bodily sensations, breathing retraining and graded exposure to feared situations

A panic attack is defined in DSM-IV as a 'discrete period in which there is the sudden onset of intense apprehension, fearfulness, or terror, often associated with feelings of impending doom'. During these attacks symptoms such as shortness of breath, palpitations, chest pain or discomfort, smothering sensations, and fear of 'going crazy' or losing control are present. Agoraphobia is anxiety about, or avoidance of, places or situations from which escape might be difficult (or embarrassing) or in which help may not be available in the event of a panic attack or panic-like symptoms. If a person avoids the situations in which panic attacks have occurred in the past for fear of encountering the same sensations, then agoraphobia can develop. In clinical settings, almost all individuals (over 95 per cent) who present with agoraphobia also have a history, or current diagnosis, of Panic Disorder.

Historically focus has been on the treatment of agoraphobia (Mathews et al., 1981) and only more recently on the treatment of panic attacks (Clark and Ehlers, 1993). The traditional approach to the treatment of agoraphobia is one of gradual exposure to feared situations. A 'ladder' is constructed with the client's major goal constituting the top rung of the ladder – for example, to be able to travel to town alone and shop there – and the bottom rung is a task which the client believes can be fairly easily accomplished – for example, walk to the end of the garden path. In collaboration with the client, possible intermediate rungs are pencilled in. The client attempts to climb one rung of the ladder between sessions, practising the step a number of times in the week. The client's progress is reviewed in the next counselling session. It is important to inoculate the client against failure experiences by stressing that the size of any step is no more than an informed guess and that it may well prove necessary to introduce intermediate rungs. Though this traditional approach is overtly behavioural it does contain implicit cognitive elements in that, essentially, clients are being asked not to personalise failure experiences. Relatives or friends may be involved as 'trainers' to ensure the client practises adequately and receives encouragement outside the counselling session. This treatment strategy is sufficiently straightforward such that it can be applied in a group format or at a distance over the telephone after an initial assessment and explanation.

Increasingly agoraphobic programmes are being extended to include a more explicitly cognitive component which focuses on the panic attacks. The cognitive theory of panic (Clark and Ehlers, 1993) states that individuals who experience panic attacks do so because they have a tendency to interpret certain bodily sensations in a catastrophic fashion. For example, perceiving a slight feeling of breathlessness as evidence that they are going to choke to death, or perceiving palpitations as evidence of an impending heart attack. This catastrophic misinterpretation of bodily sensations itself produces a worsening of the physical sensations which leads to an even more alarming interpretation and so a vicious circle is set up. There are several ways in which biological factors might increase an individual's vulnerability to the vicious circle. For example, as a consequence of normal physiological variation some individuals may experience more frequent, or more intense, benign fluctuations in body state than others. This biological factor could markedly increase the number of potential triggers for a panic attack in an individual.

A number of treatment strategies have been developed on the basis of this cognitive theory of panic disorder and they are given below.

Challenge catastrophic misinterpretations of bodily sensations

One of the commonest misinterpretations is that the palpitations clients experience are actually signs of an impending heart attack. Often these clients have had repeated reassurance from their GP that there is nothing wrong with their heart and they can be reluctant to admit even to the counsellor that they do not really believe the GP. Assuming that the client has been medically cleared, the counsellor can suggest an experiment to test out the truth of the matter by, for example, having the client repeatedly step on and off a chair until his or her calf muscles ache and then asking the client 'How is it this has not brought on a heart attack if your heart is in a weakened state?' The strategy is, again, for the client to process the data centrally rather than the counsellor to provide reassurance which could be peripherally processed by the client and dismissed. The client can then be encouraged to collect further data on his or her heart status by, for example, running up and down stairs daily at home.

A further common misinterpretation of panic clients is that they are going to faint. It is a useful starting point to ask them how many times they had predicted that they were going to faint and how many times it had actually happened. The two numbers can be written on a card to be carried with them as a reminder that they almost never get their catastrophic prediction correct. Most of these clients are unaware that in order to faint blood pressure has to drop whereas in anxiety and panic blood pressure goes up. Clients can be instructed to check their pulse or heart rate when they begin to panic. The fact that these are increasing is a sign that their blood pressure is going up and that they therefore cannot faint. Nevertheless, clients still require an explanation of the 'fainting sensation', which can be given in terms of the 'fight or flight' response. It can be explained that when a person puts a 'Danger' label on a situation, as a matter of survival the body distributes the maximum amount of energy to the muscles in order to 'fight' or run away from ('fly') the threat. This means that there is a small drop in oxygen to the brain and consequently they feel faint.

Explore the possibility that hyperventilation may be a pathway to the panic attacks and teach controlled breathing

Hyperventilation occurs when the amount of air breathed exceeds the metabolic demand for oxygen. It is often associated with fast breathing or voluminous breathing (that is, large volumes of air per cycle of inhalation and exhalation) but these do not necessarily produce hyperventilation. For example, while running or climbing the stairs a person may be engaged in both fast and voluminous breathing but not be hyperventilating if breathing supplies no more than the amount of oxygen required for the movement of large muscles. On the other hand a sedentary person watching an emotionally arousing television drama might show no signs of either fast or voluminous breathing but would be hyperventilating if the amount of air breathed exceeds the metabolic need for oxygen for maintenance of a relaxed musculature. One of the most disconcerting aspects of panic attacks is that they sometimes occur uncued, for example while relaxed or asleep, and hyperventilation is a possible explanatory mechanism for such attacks.

The first step in demonstrating to the client that hyperventilation may be playing a part in his or her difficulties is to ask the client to breathe deeply and quickly for 45 seconds. (This should not be attempted if the client has heart problems, is diabetic or pregnant.) The client is then asked what symptoms, if any, are experienced. If the client reports no symptoms the client is asked to repeat the procedure for a further 45 seconds. About 60 per cent of clients report symptoms that are somewhat similar to those produced in panic attacks, but less intense. The counsellor can then suggest that the client's breathing is implicated in the panic attacks and that had this overbreathing continued longer the symptoms would have been even more intense. To further enhance the credibility of the breathing explanation it can be suggested that the client ask his or her partner or a friend to overbreathe for 45 seconds and notice how much less disturbed he or she is. Clients are usually both surprised and relieved at there being such a simple explanation for their distress, implicitly challenging many of the catastrophic interpretations they had previously made of their distress. It should be noted, however, that hyperventilation is a complex phenomenon and that some clients will not necessarily hyperventilate as a result of fast breathing but the counsellor should nevertheless continue to elaborate on the aetiological role of hyperventilation.

The next stage is to teach the client breathing retraining. First the client is asked to describe what are the first signs of the onset of a panic – for example, feeling light-headed – and to use this as a cue for controlled breathing. The simplest strategy is to ask the client to breathe in through the nose for as long as it takes to say 'One thousand' and out through the mouth for as long as it takes to say 'Two thousand' when this cue occurs. Clients should be reminded to breathe from the stomach not the chest and that the stomach should go in when breathing out and out when breathing in. It should be stressed that it may take a couple of minutes to strike up the right rhythm with the breathing routine and that they should not expect an immediate diminution in symptoms any more than they would expect themselves to be immediately able to tap out a rhythm to a tune. For homework clients should be asked to practise the controlled breathing twice a day for ten minutes. (The breathing routine may also be taught using paced audio-tapes which encourage the client to breathe at the normal level of 14.5 breaths per minute.)

The natural inclination for clients is to escape from the situation in which the panic occurs and they should be advised to stay exactly where they are and 'ride out the storm' using the breathing routine, perhaps followed by a distraction technique. The rationale for the distraction technique is that if their senses are engaged elsewhere then there cannot be the 'overfocus' on bodily sensations. For example, a client experiencing a panic attack at a supermarket might focus, say, on a can of beans on the shelf and have a dialogue of the sort 'That's a can of beans, Smells of tomato, it would make a terrible Noise if I dropped the can, the can would be cold to Touch and I can imagine the Feel of putting my hand in the can and the Taste of licking my hand afterwards'. It should be stressed that it is only anticipated that the breathing routine and the distraction technique will 'take the edge off' their anxiety and that it is not expected that they will become relaxed as a consequence. But if they congratulate themselves on influencing their anxiety that itself will contribute to a lifting of their morale.

Have the client deliberately induce uncomfortable bodily sensations and learn to tolerate them

Table 18.1 shows exercises from among those used by Craske and Barlow (1993) to teach clients to evoke possibly similar sensations to those they experienced in panic attacks. Any exercise that evokes essentially similar sensations to the panic attack is retained, and if none of the exercises produce the panic experience it is necessary to devise some idiosyncratic exercise that will.

In the counselling session the client is asked to begin one of the exercises that is anxiety evoking and to raise a hand when the first symptoms of panic begin and to continue the induction for at least 30 seconds longer in order to break the action tendency to avoid and resist the sensations. The client can then unwind using the breathing routine and challenging catastrophic interpretations of bodily sensations. The exercise is repeated in this way until it

Table 18.1   *Interoceptive exposure exercises*

Shake head from side to side	30 seconds
Place head between legs and then lift	30 seconds
Run on spot	60 seconds
Hold breath	30 seconds or as long as possible
Stare at spot on wall or own mirror image	90 seconds

Source: Craske and Barlow (1993)

produces only mild anxiety. Then the same format is applied to the succeeding exercises. Clients are asked to practise these interoceptive exercises for homework. The homework assignment can be much more difficult for clients because they may not believe themselves 'safe' performing the exercises outside of the counsellor's office. One approach here is to help clients view the safety issue as a hypothesis to be tested out rather than a fact. The counsellor may also choose to gradually increase the number of interoceptive exercises performed for homework. The final stage of interoceptive exposure is to identify those naturally occurring triggers for the sensations they experienced in the exercises. The triggers are arranged on a ladder from least to most difficult and between sessions they are asked to tackle at least one rung three times before the next counselling session.

Key point

Catastrophic misinterpretations of bodily sensations, hyper-ventilation and intolerance of discomfort are prime targets in counselling clients with panic disorder. Agoraphobic avoidance of varying degrees is the common accompaniment of panic attacks and is tackled by graded exposure to the feared situations.

---

19 Teach the socially phobic client that others do not have 'insider knowledge' of him/her

Social phobia is a persistent fear of social or performance situations in which the person is exposed to possible scrutiny by others. The individuals fears acting in ways that are humiliating or embarrassing. The feared social or performance situations are avoided or else are endured with intense anxiety or distress.

Clark (1994) has suggested that social phobics use their interoceptive experiences to construct how others see them. This may explain the modest effects of exposure based counselling for social phobics in that they do not really process what is happening, they are responding to their construction of themselves and focusing on how they might most quickly escape.

Social phobics have a basic assumption that they do not have what it takes to make contact with the public either in limited contexts such as eating or drinking out of the home, or in a wide range of contexts such as at work or out socially at all. In support of the basic assumption a confirmation bias exists so that any hint of criticism or impaired performance is dwelt upon. Social phobics often believe that they lack basic social skills. Their belief in their ineptness is often derived from the intensity of their discomfort in social situations and an exaggerated weighting being given to verbal as opposed to non-verbal skills.

The first step in counselling the social phobic is to provide the client with a coherent rationale. One such is the metaphor of an 'out of body experience in the operating room'. It is explained that when meeting people whom clients fear will scrutinise them they do not actually engage in a dialogue with another, instead they are having a conversation with 'another self' who is located on the ceiling (the 'out of body' experience). This other self has X-ray eyes and is making inferences based on inside knowledge – for example, 'You are beginning to blush, you are going to go redder and redder' and evaluations 'You will not be able to stand the embarrassment, it will be awful'. The conversation with the other self serves to distract from interaction with another person resulting in the missing of social cues, and when these mistakes are noted by the client they are taken as evidence of social incompetence.

The second step is to teach the client to marginalise 'the self on the ceiling' by a planned ignoring of its comments in the way one would calmly ignore the ravings of a toddler having a tantrum and to visualise the bringing of this 'other self' back in the body as a prelude to focusing on the contents of the conversation with another person. Clients can be encouraged to concentrate on the contents of their interaction with others by having them summarise and reflect back what the other person has said.

Key point

Social phobics construct a picture of themselves in terms of their inside knowledge about themselves and believe that it is this person that others are interacting with. The individual's excessive criticism of this constructed self serves to distract attention from the social interaction.

---

20 Shift the post-traumatic stress disordered client's focus from the perceptual details of the trauma to a 'Yes . . . but . . . ' conceptualisation

Post-traumatic stress disorder (PTSD) was only first defined as a disorder in 1980 by the American Psychiatric Association, but terms such as 'shell shock' had long been used to describe the particular cluster of symptoms experienced by those who underwent an extreme trauma. PTSD symptoms cluster under the following three headings:

1   persistent re-experiencing of the event;

2 persistent avoidance of stimuli associated with the event;
3 persistent symptoms of increased arousal.

These symptoms have to have lasted more than one month (if the symptoms have lasted less than a month and occur within four weeks of the traumatic event, acute stress disorder is the appropriate diagnostic label). Acute PTSD is diagnosed if duration of symptoms is less than three months and chronic PTSD if duration of symptoms is three months or more. Delayed onset PTSD is specified if onset of symptoms is at least six months after the stressor.

However PTSD is an unusual disorder in that it is not totally defined by its symptoms, clients also have to meet the stressor criterion which acts as the gateway to the condition. In DSM-IV the stressor criterion (criterion A) is defined as follows:

A The person has been exposed to a traumatic event in which both of the following were present:
   1 the person experienced, witnessed, or was confronted with an event or events that involved actual or threatened death or serious injury, or a threat to the physical integrity of self or others
   2 the person's response involved intense fear, helplessness, or horror.

PTSD is classified as an anxiety disorder in DSM-IV and many of the counselling strategies for anxious clients such as graded exposure to feared situations are appropriate for PTSD clients. There is, however, considerable co-morbidity with this condition in that clients are often at least moderately depressed and may also develop a substance abuse problem. Consequently, a too narrow focus on the trauma is likely to be ineffective. There is an understandable outpouring of concern for those who undergo an extreme trauma but active interventions in the wake of a trauma should be tempered by the knowledge that not every victim suffers acute stress disorder (for example, about 90 per cent of rape victims suffer from acute stress disorder), further by no means all those who develop acute PTSD go on to develop chronic PTSD (for example, approximately one half of rape victims who suffer from acute PTSD go on to suffer from the chronic condition).

When a trauma occurs it enters working memory where there are two stores, a visual-spatial store where details of the incident are stored and a verbal store in which a description of the trauma is encoded. Details of the trauma are processed by the central executive, also in working memory, which decides on the action implications of the recently stored memory. The central executive makes a provisional decision either to take flight from the scene of the trauma or to fight the trauma. This 'fight–flight' response is accompanied by physiological arousal in which oxygen is diverted to the body's major muscles leaving the brain slightly short of oxygen resulting in light-headedness. When the immediate trauma has passed the central executive conducts a reappraisal in which it examines whether the incident really constituted such a threat, whether there have been similar incidents in the past, and the likelihood of such incidents in the future. The judgement of the central executive on these matters may be influenced by the opinions of others and by whether the central executive part of working memory was itself damaged in the trauma.

The decision of the central executive is thus essentially two-fold between vigilance and hypervigilance. In the former it is conceded that danger is a possibility but in the latter condition it is assumed everything is dangerous. The distinction between vigilance and hypervigilance can be exemplified by an analogy, imagine your home has been burgled (trauma): a vigilant response would be to install a burglar alarm whereas the hypervigilant response would be to set it so sensitively that it is triggered when heavy wagons pass down the road. In the hypervigilant state the central executive essentially closes down and is dictated to by the contents of the verbal and visual-spatial stores, reversing the normal hierarchy. That is, perceptual processing continues to dominate the person's behaviour, by, for example, seeking out physical matches to the details of the trauma as opposed to conceptual processing in which there is an objective determination of the likelihood of future threat. The closing down of the central executive is experienced as a loss of control and depression usually ensues.

There are emotional, cognitive, behavioural and motivational dimensions to the hypervigilance, all of which reciprocally interact with each other. At an emotional level the dominant emotions are apprehension and depression. Behaviourally anything reminiscent of the trauma is avoided. At a cognitive level the individual replays the trauma as a way of reminding him- or herself why certain situations are avoided, operating on the maxim 'Those who do not remember history are condemned to relive it' and a set of trauma beliefs will be distilled (see the Trauma Belief Inventory; Scott and Stradling, 1992). A trauma is liable to interrupt abruptly the actions and goals of the individual. At a motivational level the person is still directed to those goals but has to contend with a system that has 'closed down for safety' and this leads to uncharacteristic irritability at an emotional level. This model accounts for all the major features of PTSD: re-experiencing, avoidance behaviour and disordered arousal.

With this model in mind the goal of counselling is to enable the client's central executive to securely attach a 'Yes . . . but . . . ' label to the memory of the trauma. That is, the client is enabled to say 'YES it is horrific that it happened, I can still see the horror BUT the trauma has to be viewed in the wider context of my life and it is of doubtful relevance for . . . '.

Key point

Post-traumatic stress disorder has three symptom clusters: re-experiencing the trauma, avoidance of anything associated with the trauma, and disordered arousal – such as uncharacteristic irritability, impaired concentration, sleep difficulties. The disorder is a response to a reappraisal of the trauma in which it is decided it is safest to assume danger is everywhere and abandon any attempt to centrally process data from the environment or from the verbal and visual-spatial stores in which the memory of the trauma resides. The goal of counselling is to enable the client to 'Yes . . . but . . . ' the trauma.

---

21   Normalise the PTSD client's response to the trauma and together distil an adaptive interpretation of the event(s)

Clients suffering from PTSD can be much reassured by describing their symptoms as a normal response to an abnormal situation. It is useful to suggest that as a consequence of the trauma their 'alarm' in the nervous system is set oversensitively and they are therefore experiencing many false alarms. The counselling task is one of helping them reset their alarm to a more appropriate level but this can only be done gradually.

A major focus will be on them controlling their traumatic memory, rather than for it to control them. That is, the client must become able to switch from perceptual processing of the trauma to conceptual processing. During the initial period of confrontation with the trauma it is clearly more advantageous to know the physical surroundings, what escape routes might be possible, whether energy should be deployed on a particular route, rather than to be concerned with conceptual issues such as how likely it is for the trauma to occur in the future. After the trauma, however, it is important that conceptual processing comes to dominate.

Counselling begins with helping the client reappraise the trauma. Clients will usually furnish the counsellor with a description of their trauma but it is most often an edited version. Usually there are aspects of the trauma they have told no one about because of the horror which those aspects evoke. As part of the assessment process it is useful to gauge the severity of PTSD using the PENN Inventory (Hammarberg, 1992) and the Impact of Events Scale (Horowitz et al., 1979) (these questionnaires are reproduced in Scott and Stradling, 1992). The PENN has a question that provides a clue as to whether the client may be withholding some information. To Question 12 the client has to make one of the following responses:

0 'I've told a friend or family member about the important part of my most traumatic experiences.'
1 'I've had to be careful in choosing the parts of my traumatic experiences to tell friends or family members.'
2 'Some parts of my traumatic experiences are so hard to understand that I've said almost nothing about them to anyone.'
3 'No one could possibly understand the traumatic experiences I've had to live with.'

The client should be asked to elaborate further if the response is either of the last three (that is, with a score above zero), the rationale here being that one can ultimately only reappraise something if one first acknowledges what one believed that something to be. However, great care needs to be taken over the pace with which the counsellor seeks this elaboration, as there is a serious danger of overwhelming the client and thus the client quickly defaulting from treatment. At the other extreme salient material may be totally left out of reappraisal.

During the counselling sessions the client biases in appraising their trauma (shown in Table 21.1) can be noted and more realistic interpretations discussed (from Scott and Stradling, 1992: 43).

Table 21.1 *Cognitive biases in environmental appraisal*

All or nothing thinking: Everything is seen in black and white terms, for example, 'I am either in control of what's happening to me or I am not'.

Overgeneralisation: Expecting a uniform response from a category of people because of the misdeeds of a member, for example 'All men are rapists'.

Mental filter: Seizing on a negative fragment of a situation and dwelling on it, for example 'I could have been killed in that encounter'.

Automatic discounting: Brushing aside the positive aspects of what was achieved in a trauma, for example 'I was only doing my duty in saving the child'.

Jumping to conclusions: Assuming that it is known what others think, for example 'They all think I should be over it by now, it was six weeks ago after all'.

Magnification and minimisation: Magnification of shortcomings and minimisation of strengths, for example 'Since the trauma I am so irritable with the family and just about manage to keep going to work'.

Emotional reasoning: Focusing on emotional state to draw conclusions about oneself, for example 'Since it happened, I am frightened of my own shadow, I guess I am just a wimp'.

'Should' statements: Inappropriate use of moral imperatives – 'shoulds', 'musts', 'haves', and 'oughts'; for example 'Its ridiculous that since the attack I now have to take my daughter with me shopping. I should be able to go by myself'.

Labelling and mislabelling: For example, 'I used to think of myself as a strong person. I could handle anything, but since it happened I am just weak'.

Personalisation: Assuming that because something went wrong it must be your fault, for example 'I keep going over my handling of the situation. I must have made a mistake somewhere for the child to have died'.

The biases illustrated in Table 21.1 in information processing are also in evidence in the common accompaniment of PTSD – depression. Earlier, cognitive restructuring procedures were described for depression and anxiety and these are equally applicable to PTSD (see Scott and Stradling, 1992). Because of the considerable co-morbidity associated with PTSD the counsellor tackling these clients needs a familiarity with treating a wide range of disorders and problems.

One particular concern is that many victims of extreme trauma become uncharacteristically irritable, causing relationship problems with the family and friends who are trying to support the client. The client and his or her 'supporters' may come to exceed each other's tolerance thresholds, creating a vicious circle. It is useful to explain to the partner not to take the client's uncharacteristic irritability personally. One way of helping the client break the circle is by teaching the 'traffic light' routine. Clients often find it useful when experiencing the first symptoms of anger to visualise a set of traffic lights on red, and shout 'STOP!' to themselves. As the lights turn to amber they ask themselves 'Am I absolutely sure they did it deliberately just to wind me up? And is it really the end of the world if they did?' Then as the lights go to green they move to another room to calm down and distract themselves with something pleasant.

The proximal cause of the PTSD client's irritability is an identifiable event in the present – for example, annoyance at a child putting down a hot drink on a polished surface – but the remote or distal cause may relate to the client's frustration at the inability to pursue pre-trauma actions and goals. Matters are compounded if the client believes that the pre-trauma actions and goals are the only route to happiness, and that it is 'Not fair' that previous activities have had to be relinquished. These beliefs should be challenged through Socratic dialogue.

The PTSD client has a pressing need to understand how the trauma fits into his or her life, yet consideration of it is so distressing that it militates against finding an answer. Historically, cognitive-behavioural treatment of PTSD has gone against the natural grain of the client, which is to avoid thinking about the trauma, by advocating, typically, hour long, daily, imaginal exposures to the memory or *in vivo* exposures. The published studies with this exposure rationale are, however, problematic in that either there have been no checks to verify that clients actually did their homeworks and in the way prescribed, or they were atypical PTSD clients being only mildly depressed and/or media recruited. Because these exposure therapies are against the grain for most clients they are liable, in routine practice, to generate high levels of non-compliance and defaulting. It may also be argued that it is not in any case habituation – that is, progressive decrements in response to memories of the trauma – that should be the prime concern but rather promoting adaptive interaction with the memory.

There are a number of ways of getting the client to interact adaptively with the memory of the trauma. The reappraisal can begin by asking the client to write about the trauma for ten minutes each day. It is helpful if the client tackles the writing at a fixed time otherwise, because of its onerous nature, it quickly becomes a victim of circumstances. Clients do, however, need careful preparation for this homework exercise because they will have expended a considerable amount of energy in trying not to think about the trauma and the counsellor seems to be suggesting doing the opposite. The counsellor must determine beforehand whether the client believes this is a viable homework exercise, if not it will need adjusting. With one elderly survivor of the D-Day landings in 1944 the first author had to be content with one sentence a day! Further the counsellor should point out that certainly in the first week of writing the client may be more distressed but as the writing continues alternative perspectives will suggest themselves and the client will become less distressed.

This procedure may well suffice with cases of acute PTSD but chronic cases usually require extra work. The writings of the client may be dictated onto an audio-tape and the client is asked to listen to it on a daily basis, again at a fixed time. Clients are asked to keep a note of which aspect of the tape was most distressing to them on a particular day, using a scale from 0 to 10 where 10 is the most distressing. Interestingly, what distresses a client most one day is not what causes most distress another day, suggesting that a reappraisal process is the active mechanism involved. Understandably clients are tempted to switch off the tape at the worst point but the counsellor should stress to the client that it is important to control the memory rather than for the memory to control the client and that therefore the client must not switch off the tape until he or she is less distressed than at the worst point. Thus if the worst point on a particular day occurred at the end of the tape the client must rewind it and play it until feeling less distressed. It cannot be stressed too strongly to clients that they must not distract themselves from their trauma tape, particularly the most distressing aspects, because this will pre-clude an alternative interpretation.

Some clients, though unwilling to write about their trauma, may be willing to record details on an audio-tape in the presence of the counsellor and then listen to the tape at home. However, some clients, particularly the more severely depressed, are unwilling to use a trauma tape. As an alternative the client and counsellor can distil six statements which comprehensively cover the trauma, each of the statements typically two or three sentences long. Each statement is, as it were, put on a slide so that the client can visualise it and each 'slide' is visualised for 30 seconds before progressing on to the next. Thus one full sequence of the slides would take just three minutes. Clients are then asked what is the longest period of time they could see themselves going through the slides for and they typically reply 'About ten minutes'. The counsellor would then suggest going through the sequence at least twice a day. This, on the one hand, maximises the likelihood that the client will have the opportunity to reappraise the trauma, while at the same time ensuring it is a success experience. Clients' compliance with the reappraisal process can be enhanced by involving their partner in the counselling.

The strategies discussed above all involve scheduling a time at which the concerns raised by the trauma are addressed. In practice, of course, PTSD clients feel that trauma issues dominate their waking and sleeping hours, but even this degree of contemplation is ineffective because the central executive is largely inoperative. To help restore the supremacy of the central executive outside these scheduled times it is helpful to teach clients a 'merry-go-round' strategy. This involves clients 'catching' trauma-related thoughts and images and placing them on a merry-go-round visualised as being located outside the clients' heads and at some distance from them. They are told that as they go about their daily business they cannot but help seeing the trauma thoughts and images come around on the merry-go-round, but when this happens they are simply to acknowledge them with a passing nod in their direction and carry on with what they were doing. Continuing the metaphor, clients are told that if they persist with simply nodding to the thoughts and images the merry-go-round slows down and the frequency of intrusions thereby reduces. Further, it is suggested that times of maximum distress are probably those in which they have boarded the merry-go-round, having become engaged in arguing with or attempting to brush aside some aspect of the trauma. In these instances they must visualise themselves detaching from the merry-go-round, then distancing from it, and finally resuming a 'nodding terms' relationship with the memory of the trauma.

Key point

Care has to be taken that the client ultimately reappraises a comprehensive version of the trauma but not at a pace which would lead to disengagement from counselling. Cognitive restructuring is important both for the PTSD itself and for the associated anxiety, depression and irritability.

---

22   Teach the client with obsessive-compulsive disorder a radical apathy for disturbing thoughts and response prevention for ritual behaviour

Obsessive-compulsive disorder is characterised by obsessions which cause marked anxiety or distress and/or by compulsions which serve to neutralise anxiety. Among the most common obsessions are repeated thoughts about contamination, repeated doubts such as about whether one has actually dropped something, and a need to have things in a particular order. Compulsions are repetitive behaviours – for example, hand washing – or mental acts – such as repeating words silently – the goal of which is to prevent or reduce anxiety or distress. This diagnosis is only applied to adults if at some point they have recognised that the obsessions or compulsions are excessive or unreasonable.

Compulsive behaviours have traditionally been tackled by exposure to the feared stimuli and response prevention, that is prevention of compulsive rituals and neutralising behaviours. Thus, for example, clients who engaged in ritual hand washing would be encouraged to wash their hands once and then to immediately switch to another behaviour such as eating a meal but to do so without engaging in an internal dialogue in which they agonise about whether they 'Really are safe'. Instead they simply carry their fear with them which diminishes over time.

The counselling session is used to practise tolerance of the fear that the stimulus evokes. Thus a client obsessed with the possibility of contamination might be asked to replace the emptied contents of the counsellor's litter bin. Before the exercise the client would be asked to rate his or her fear on a scale from 0 to 100 – which might be, say, 80 – then to rate the fear when actually touching the contents – say 95 – (at which point the client will experience an extreme desire to wash), then every ten minutes the client would be asked for another fear or desire-to-escape score. Typically over the period of an hour there is a marked decrement in fear to around 60, and the conversation with the counsellor is prolonged until there is a marked decrement. It should be noted, however, that the counsellor does not engage in any reassurance in this period – if the contamination fears are addressed by the counsellor it simply feeds the obsession. Clients should be asked to engage in exposure as a homework assignment, seeking the habituation response. Within-session habituation makes it much more likely that an exposure homework will be attempted. Exposure to feared stimuli is conducted at each counselling session and over sessions there should be a gradual decrease in the maximum fear encountered in each session. Typically about ten counselling sessions are needed.

Where obsessive-compulsive clients doubt they have done something, such as bolted the door, it is useful to suggest that they attach an unusual imaginary label to their action such as 'black snowball'. Thus when they are tempted to check whether they have indeed bolted the door the imagery of the 'black snowball' tells them they have. The imaginary label should be changed each time they perform an action that in the past has become a ritual. In some instances it is not so much that clients check a behaviour but rather that they spend an inordinate amount of time looking at the consequences of the action they have performed, for example, staring at the knob of a cooker that they have switched off. Putting a time limit on the duration of their stare can help in these instances, followed by gradually reducing the time allowed.

Part of the difficulty for many obsessives is that they do not know that they know something, that is, their deficiencies are at a meta-level. They can be reassured by telling them that there are two forms of knowledge, procedural and declarative. When a person first learns something everything has to be spelt out and verbalised, for example when learning to drive the novice uses declarative knowledge which is effortful and exhausting. With practice the techniques become proceduralised (procedural knowledge) and automated so that ten years after passing the driving test the car driver drives effortlessly from A to B and would have difficulty explaining to a novice the detail of how this had actually been done.

It is useful to think of procedural knowledge as a reference library which obviates the need to be able to spell out actions after an initial learning period. For example one client felt compelled to read over and over the instructions on packets of soup. When he picked up a soup packet he was instructed to shout 'Stop, it's in my library' and to make the soup without reading. To highlight how the overuse of declarative knowledge impairs performance, a male client could be asked to put a tie on (which most do very quickly – procedural knowledge) and the client is asked to instruct the counsellor in how to put a tie on, which is more fraught and takes longer (declarative knowledge). An analogy can be made with breathing: just as clients trust themselves to breathe so they have to trust that their actions and judgements will be governed by their 'library'.

The issue of trust also arises in the context of obsessive-compulsive disordered clients' relationships with other people where they may be unable to trust their judgement that they have not been negligent towards or harmed another person. Their difficulty arises because they insist on working at a declarative level where the details of their actions are assembled and expect the 'facts' to somehow speak for themselves. It is argued that judgements are, however, largely a product of the procedural library which takes into account the person's long learning history, such that in the domain in question products of the procedural library are regarded as 'alien' and dismissed. Instead there is a preoccupation with the declarative – for example, 'Did I really check that every food at the children's party did not contain harmful additives? I checked the food I bought but did I check Jane's food? I feel so guilty.' It is important for counsellors and relatives not to join the client at this declarative level, as this perpetuates the mistaken belief that only this level exists. In the presence of the client, his or her partner and family should be dissuaded from giving reassurance, operating on the maxim 'I will say this only once'.

It is very easy to be seduced by obsessive-compulsive disorder clients into thinking that the central problem is a 'proper' consideration of the details, perhaps getting the opinions of an ever growing body of experts. In practice they will alternate their pseudo-judgements almost by the minute. The counselling task is to help them view these oscillations at a distance and with a radical apathy.

Some cases of obsessive-compulsive disorder do not have compulsive behaviours, rather they experience an intrusive repetitive thought that they are going to do something shameful or harmful. It will probably need to be explained to the client that it is specific plans that lead to actions, not thoughts or images about action. Clients can be asked to put the contents of their obsession on audio-tape and listen to it on a daily basis for as long as it takes to be significantly less troubled than at their worst point. It is important that they do not try to produce counter arguments to their obsessional thoughts but rather develop a 'So what?' response. Clients can also be asked to detach themselves from their obsessive thoughts by 'catching' them when they occur and mentally placing them on a roundabout located across a 'moat' outside their head. When they catch sight of the obsessive thought on the roundabout they are asked to visualise themselves waving to the thought and to continue to experience reality by following the rhythm of their breathing. They are asked to neither get involved with the thoughts by crossing the moat and boarding the roundabout, nor to 'throw bricks at it' or 'run away'.

Key point

For checking behaviours the client can mentally attach a 'strange label'. Once the client has performed the activity, this serves as a reminder when the urge to repeat the behaviour occurs, encouraging response prevention. The counsellor should encourage the client not to argue with obsessive thoughts but to treat them with apathy as just intrusive thoughts which do not carry action implications.

IV Common Problems

23 Tackle partners' non-acceptance of or addiction to each other

Cognitive-behavioural couples therapy has been found to improve relationship quality for approximately two-thirds of couples presenting for counselling (Jacobsen et al., 1987). Traditionally this has involved behavioural contracts such as 'John agrees to come home from work on time and Jan agrees not to greet him with a complaint', and communication training (see Scott, 1989). Couples therapy is also an effective way of treating depression (O'Leary and Beach, 1990) as there is a high degree of overlap between severe depression and marital discord.

However, clinical experience suggests the most common scenario is that the counsellor is presented with a client who cites a partner as the major cause of distress and adds that the latter would be unwilling to attend counselling. It is possible to affect the quality of the couple's relationship with only one partner present, though this is not ideal. The client typically presents his or her distress as an inevitable response to the behaviour of the partner. The cognitive-behavioural model however asserts that distress is for the most part a consequence of a particular interpretation of a behaviour. The first step is then to enquire whether the behaviours complained about have always been viewed as so problematic. If there was a stage when the problem was labelled mildly problematic, it is important to discover what thought processes and behaviours made it possible to then accept the behaviour. The issue of possible acceptance becomes a major focus when the other partner is unable or unwilling to change.

There are two questions the counsellor needs to ask. The first is 'What made you more able to tolerate this behaviour earlier?' The answer might be that the client offset the partner's behaviour by engaging in some uplifting activity. In some instances it is possible to raise a person's tolerance threshold by the reintroduction of the activity. For example John had survived his wife's frequent temper tantrums until he retired when he gave into her carping criticisms of his hobby, photography, and sold his camera and equipment. Once he decided to re-engage in his old activities he found he was again able to weather her tirades. On occasion it is actually the case that the complained about behaviour was actually once seen in a vaguely positive light. For example, Jane, a rather shy client, now complaining bitterly about her husband's drink problem, had once thought 'It was nice that everyone at our local knew and liked Jim and no one would hear a word said against him'. Where the behaviour was seen somewhat positively it is useful to have the client elaborate on the details to enable him or her to express some of the softer emotions towards the partner. This is not to negate the current negative impact of the behaviour but to encourage acknowledgement of the partner's positive attributes which, in turn, improves motivation.

The second question is 'What led you to see the behaviour as particularly problematic now?' This often reflects a social comparison. For example Peter had been married twenty years, had five children and was totally involved in family life, but his wife had always been reckless with money. Peter had begun to feel that, compared with his colleagues, he was missing out on life. He, unlike them, could not easily afford to go to a rugby match and have a few drinks afterwards, and he began the counselling session complaining bitterly about his wife's mismanagement of money. Recently they had had an argument in a supermarket because he had taken some items out of the shopping trolley and placed them back on the shelves. His wife would not come to counselling because she did not see that she had a problem nor could she understand why Peter should bother. After a number of counselling sessions Peter said 'I used to think she was the problem, but she is not. I am the one who has changed, it will be easier if I just accept her. It worked for years.' The counsellor had tried in vain to get Peter to do things independently for himself but found that he was amenable to, and benefited from, a 'special time' each week with his wife away from the children.

A change in social comparison can have led a client to dislike intensely his or her own behaviour but feel powerless to change it. The client's misery may be compounded by a partner's 'justified' criticism of this behaviour. The way forward with such cases is to help the client accept that, at least initially, there will be a gap between private feelings and public behaviour and not to apologise for this gap. For example Keith sought help for his lack of demonstrativeness with his wife and two young children. He had come to dislike intensely the coldness of his family of origin and to appreciate the warmth of his wife's family. Nevertheless he seemed unable to show his affection. Upon closer examination of his interactions it emerged that if he greeted his wife's family in their customary way with a hug he inwardly cringed. Then he would get angry with himself for the feelings and over time he had avoided hugs in order to avoid the feelings. The counselling task was to encourage him to accept his feelings and not turn them into a moral issue and to engage in the public behaviours he believed were appropriate.

A similar issue arises when partners are reunited after one of them has been unfaithful. The unfaithful partner may show all the consideration that was perhaps previously lacking but the faithful partner is bedevilled by thoughts of 'How can I ever trust him or her again?', with occasional outbursts of anger over trivia which are then followed by guilt because the unfaithful partner is now doing everything that could be expected. The counselling strategy is to help the faithful partner accept that his or her feelings are bound to be mixed. On the one hand the client cannot see into the future and cannot be certain the unfaithfulness will not happen again, and on the other hand there is the evidence that the unfaithful partner is obviously trying. Clients often take mixed feelings as evidence that they are 'mixed up' which they then berate themselves for. They can be helped to accept their mix of feelings by suggesting that it is as if they have a clouded crystal ball in their left hand and sometimes they turn to it and try and peer into it, while on other occasions in their right hand they are watching a video of their partner's current behaviour. Depending on whether they turn to the left or turn to the right they will inevitably experience almost momentary changes of feelings. The client's task is to make the best of the current day given the hurts that are around.

In some cases the client has virtually always seen the behaviour of the partner as problematic yet continues the relationship. It can be useful to have the client complete a decision matrix on the advantages and disadvantages of separating both in the short and long term. Often the financial or housing difficulties of a separation, or the interruption of the children's schooling, are cited as reasons for the continuance of the relationship.

When clients allow these reasons to determine their behaviour it is often the case that they have a long-term difficulty first of acknowledging their own needs and second of giving themselves permission to meet their own needs. Such clients present as 'victims', the counsellor is auditioned for the impossible role of 'rescuer' while their partner is allocated the role of 'persecutor'. The counsellor can begin to encourage clients out of the victim role by suggesting that their present course of action is itself a specific choice, that they are not helpless, and that to do nothing is itself a choice. The encouragement to relinquish the victim role should be done alongside activity scheduling. The client can become committed to activity scheduling by the counsellor's use of metaphor, for example, 'Doesn't Cinderella have a right to go to the ball?' Focusing prematurely and exclusively on giving up the victim role means the counsellor is allocated a persecutor role and counselling may be prematurely terminated. Many of these clients have avoidant and/or dependent personality disorders and it is always important to enquire before the end of the counselling session whether there was anything you said that may have particularly upset them. Because of the prevalence of personality disordered clients in this population counselling is often very long term, typically bimonthly sessions over a number of years. Over this period of time and with this scheduling of sessions the client's self-esteem can be improved by the counsellor accepting and respecting the 'choices' the client has made but without dependency developing. Additionally the continued activity scheduling develops an implicit belief that the client does have a right to meet his or her own needs. The stage is then set for the client to revise the original decision about the relationship.

Clients are sometimes referred to counsellors to help them cope with a recent separation from their partner. In such instances the counsellor is often asked impossible questions like 'Do you think they will ever come back?' and the task is then to accept the pain that lies behind the question rather than hazard an answer. Initially the counsellor's strategies need to be more emotion focused. But as time progresses one can gently question whether the absent partner was as desirable as at first implied. This can serve as a prelude to questioning whether living with that particular partner has to be the only route to happiness. If the client continues to insist that the absent partner is the only route to happiness the counsellor can introduce the notion that perhaps the client was addicted to the partner rather than loved the partner and that what the client is currently experiencing are withdrawal symptoms. This can be exemplified in the distinction between 'want' and 'need'. Clients may want a particular partner but they do not need them, and it is possible to become at least just reasonably content with life even if some of our wants are not met.

> **Key point**
>
> When only one partner of a distressed dyad will present for counselling that partner often casts him- or herself in the role of victim, the absent partner as persecutor and the counsellor is auditioned for the role of rescuer. The counselling task is to help the client give up the victim role and explore if and why the complained about behaviour has only recently become so objectionable. This can result in the development of acceptance as an adaptive coping strategy. In cases where the partner's behaviour has always been objectionable it can be suggested that the client might want to work on overcoming the 'addiction' to the partner but, as with all addictions, there will be withdrawal symptoms.

24 Assess and enhance the suitability of the addicted client for a cognitive-behavioural counselling programme

Clients presenting with addictive behaviours vary greatly in their motivation for tackling their addiction. At one extreme there are the 'pre-contemplators' (Prochaska and DiClemente, 1984) who see no reason to tackle their addiction, and agree to see the counsellor largely as a means of placating others or as part of the conditions for acquiring a legal substitute for a drug. Somewhat more motivated are the 'contemplators' who see advantages and disadvantages of tackling their addiction. When the advantages of tackling the addiction outweigh the disadvantages the person will enter the next motivational phase, 'action', in which attempts are made to curb the substance consumption.

The traditional cognitive-behavioural counselling approach of regular sessions over a limited period with follow up booster sessions is only likely to be applicable to the more motivated client. Both clients and counsellors become frustrated if this model is imposed on all addicts. The most appropriate response is to have an 'opt in' procedure in which the person is asked two questions on a questionnaire:

1   Do you think that you would benefit from a series of regular counselling sessions to help you sort out your drug problem? Please underline one of the following:

   No, not at all
   It's very unlikely
   Possibly
   Definitely

2   If you responded 'possibly' or 'definitely' to the above question, how likely is it that you would turn up to most of the sessions? Please underline one of the following:

   No chance
   Very unlikely
   Quite likely
   Very likely

These two questions tap the two most important determinants of subsequent behaviour. First a person's belief in whether the behaviour is worthwhile (outcome expectations) and second the person's belief in his or her ability to perform a behaviour (self-efficacy). Those who answer 'possibly/definitely' and 'quite likely/very likely' should be considered for assignment to weekly counselling sessions over a three-month period followed by booster sessions over the following year. The questionnaire should, of course, be complemented with an interview in which the counsellor tries to determine the client's level of motivation. This is best achieved by helping clients articulate for themselves their areas of concern and their arguments for change. It is vital in so doing that the counsellor does not put words into the client's mouth. Thus the counsellor would begin with a question of the sort 'How do drugs fit into your life?' as opposed to 'What problems do drugs cause you?' which invites a display of motivation. Only after the *client* has defined something as a problem can the counsellor use the term, otherwise the assessment process becomes prejudiced.

   For the less motivated client an open door policy may be more appropriate where the client can attend during a crisis. Rollnick et al. (1992) have described brief motivational interviewing strategies, shown in Table 24.1, that might be more appropriate with this population.

   Using Table 24.1 the counsellor would begin contact with the

Table 24.1   *Strategies for use with pre-contemplators and contemplators*

A   *Strategies for use with pre-contemplators*

1   Opening strategy: life-style, stresses and substance use
2   Opening strategy: health and substance use
3   A typical day/session

B   *Strategies for use with contemplators*

4   The good things and the less good things
5   Providing information
6   The future and the present
7   Exploring concerns and decision making

client at the top of the table, simply enquiring how drugs fit into the client's life. If the client is reasonably forthcoming about this and not threatened the counsellor can move the discussion on to asking 'How does your use of (substance) affect your health?' Progression to the next step only occurs when the client has become comfortable with the previous enquiries. In this next stage the counsellor might say 'I would like to spend a couple of minutes getting a picture of your day. What happened, how did you feel, and where did your use of (substance) fit in? Let's start at the beginning.' The input from the counsellor at this stage is one of simple open questions.

Progression to stage 4 is led by the client and requires some intimation from the client of a substance concern. The counsellor's response is to underplay the concern by talking of it as one of the less good things about the substance use. This allows the client space to acknowledge openly some of the good things about the substance use. Paradoxically the client then tends to express concern with the less good things even more forcefully. This creates a context in which factual information about the substance use can be presented by the counsellor and centrally processed by the client. The premature provision of this information would have resulted in peripheral processing by the client inviting easy dismissal.

When this information has been properly assimilated the counsellor can move on to the next stage and ask the client 'How would you like things to be different in the future?' This should be contrasted with how things are at present. The client is then helped to examine what would need to be done to 'advance his or her journey' and what 'roadblocks' (usually substance related) would be met on the way and how, if at all, the roadblocks might be circumvented. It is important at this stage to explore any concerns the client might have about no longer using as well as concerns about using. The final stage involves decision making: 'Where does this leave you now?'; 'What are you going to do?' One of the options when clients finally reach this stage is to offer a structured problem solving programme.

Key point

Assess which addicted clients are more suitable for an open door or crisis intervention strategy and which more suitable for a structured cognitive-behavioural programme. Use motivational interviewing strategies to enhance motivation.

---

25   Offer suitably motivated clients with an addiction a problem solving programme

For the more motivated clients a problem solving programme may be used into which new drug related behaviours are introduced as options to be considered when confronted by particular problems. This takes account of the fact that many addicts may have problems beyond the drug use – indeed for some the drug use is more a consequence than a cause of problems. Six stages of problem solving are now outlined.

I   Problem orientation

It is explained that some people label every hassle as a catastrophe and so distress themselves unnecessarily. Most problems can be sorted out somehow, though rarely perfectly. It is important to stress that problem solving cannot begin until the person gives up saying to him- or herself 'I cannot stand things or people not being exactly the way I want them when I want them' or, alternatively, 'The whole world ought to be organised to meet my every need'. These statements may not be verbalised overtly but clients should be asked if it is 'as if' much of the time they are voicing these 'I can't stand it' sentiments to themselves, often accompanied by persistent complaining about something or someone. Many of those who experience difficulties with problem orientation labour under the illusion that only they have problems, and that it is 'not fair' that others do not. A variant on this theme is that they believe their experiencing of hassles is a sign of their personal inadequacy rather than as par for the course this side of the grave.

All or nothing thinking is very much associated with a deficit in problem orientation, with solutions being seen as either a perfect answer or no answer at all. This black and white thinking is very much in evidence with the significant minority of addicts who have a borderline personality disorder. The all or nothing thinking leads to very impulsive behaviour (hence the tendency to abuse substances). For example Carol was delighted she had got a job as a secretary at a college, where her problems with heroin were unknown and she felt she could make a fresh start. However, she walked out in the middle of the first morning because she was unfamiliar with the word processing package they were using and there was no one about to show her. This form of thinking also poses a problem for the counselling endeavour – either it is seen as 'superb' or as 'the pits'. Thus the counsellor can use the client's reaction to the counselling sessions themselves to illustrate and challenge the client's dichotomous thinking and thereby encourage the client to continue to engage in the counselling.

Discussion of problem orientation, that is of the importance of locking on to problems, will be a dominant feature of the earlier counselling sessions. To explain the concept it is useful to use a metaphor such as 'Problem orientation is like locating a spanner over a nut, you may have all the strength to turn the nut (that is, solve the problem) but unless it is properly positioned in the first place it will all be to no avail.' As the counsellor develops a rapport with the client it becomes more possible to challenge the often constant complaining of those with a deficit in problem orientation by asking them to sit in your seat while you sit in theirs and verbalise their complaints. This reverse role play graphically and humorously illustrates to the client the pointlessness of constantly 'awfulising'.

During the counselling programme it will again be necessary to attend to the all or nothing thinking with regard to slips. The dichotomous thinking means that slips are likely to be interpreted catastrophically which in turn leads to more taking of the substance to assuage guilt feelings. The goal is to stop the inevitable slips from becoming full blown relapses by getting the client to see a slip simply as a mistake from which something can be learned to help prevent subsequent slips.

2   Problem definition

This involves a precise definition of the client's problems in as specific a manner as possible. Thus with regard to substance abuse it is important to discover what have been the specific stimuli for the client taking the substance in the past. Common ones are negative emotional states, interpersonal conflict and social pressure.

3   Generation of alternatives

Here it is important to go for quantity rather than quality of possible solutions to the client's problems.

4   Choosing a solution or combination of solutions

This involves accepting that the chosen solution is likely to be 'on balance' the best available solution rather than waiting for a solution about which the client feels certain. Choosing a solution can be impeded by the client believing that he or she 'couldn't stand not making the right choice'. Teaching the client that he or she does not have a crystal ball and that any decision is necessarily based on incomplete data and is therefore provisional is very important. It is further necessary to make plain that the client's worth as a person does not depend on making the right decision – if this is what the client believes then he or she is likely to freeze and be unable to make a decision.

In choosing a solution it is important that the client distinguish between short- and long-term consequences. Tackling an addiction usually carries with it short-term disadvantage but long-term advantages. The short-term pain can be made more acceptable by the counsellor verbalising the client's expressed wishes about how the client would wish life to be different.

5 Planning how to implement the decision and specifying the steps in concrete terms

Many addicted clients will also be depressed and it is therefore important to implement changes in small manageable stages, so that there is a sense of achievement from one stage that gives encouragement to tackle the next stage.

6 Reviewing the chosen solution or combination of solutions in the light of experience

It may be necessary to go back to the menu of options at stage two and try one of the other solutions, or developing another solution and trying that.

One of the functions of this problem solving format is to keep the client increasingly task focused, 'What is it I have to do?', rather than engaging in constant emotional discharge, 'Isn't it awful that . . . '. The latter can serve to fuel the sensation seeking behaviour prominent with addicted clients. The goal is to achieve a proper balance of problem focused and emotion focused coping rather than have an exclusive emphasis on either one.

Each of the client's problems, both substance and non-substance related, can be tackled using the problem solving pro forma given in Table 13.3. Substance abuse often carries with it attendant practical problems such as housing, finances and so on. The pro forma is an excellent vehicle for tackling these problems and should be attempted early on in counselling. Success on these practical matters teaches the problem solving method and encourages both continued engagement in counselling and an increased preparedness to tackle the substance related matters. This will, however, require the counsellor to become familiar with locally available resources such as Housing Associations and often to be prepared to act as an advocate for the client.

Azrin et al. (1994) have described a successful treatment programme for drug abusers that involves stimulus control, urge control and competing response procedures. Each of these can be considered as specific alternative solutions that can be introduced into the problem solving framework when drug use is the problem defined. Strategies for these are now described.

1   Stimulus control procedures

This strategy is designed to eliminate external stimulus situations that were precursors to substance use and to increase situations and activities incompatible with or not associated with substance use. A 'risk list' is constructed of situations, persons and places associated with substance use. Then a 'safe list' is constructed of situations, persons and places incompatible or unassociated with substance use. A daily planner recording form is utilised to schedule only activities from the safe list for the following day. The counsellor reinforces the client for time spent in safe activities and problem solves with the client how to increase safe durations while decreasing risk durations.

2   Urge control and competing response procedures

This strategy is designed to interrupt internal stimuli (sensations, urges, thoughts or incipient actions) associated with substance use and then to substitute competing internal and external stimuli. The first step is to ask the client to close his or her eyes and recall the most recent slip. Then the client is asked to describe it in great detail up to the point where the substance related urge, thought or feeling was initially discernible. At the instant of discernibility the client has to interrupt the description by shouting 'No!' or 'Stop!' followed by brief phrases describing the negative consequences of substance use. To arrive at suitable phrases the counsellor should help the client vividly distil the two worst consequences of the substance use. It is important, however, that these two worst consequences are not too remote. For example in Alma's case her worst fears were to imagine her husband leaving her and their children being taken from her. When describing the negative consequences it is important that they are sufficiently vivid to evoke strong negative affect. After the negative affect has declined the client follows his or her rhythm of breathing saying to him- or herself 'Calm' and 'Relax' for about 5 seconds. The essence of this strategy is that it locates the client in the here and now and any urges and images are regarded as no more than images and urges so that the client achieves distance from them and they are not seen as auto-matically carrying implications for action. This is followed by the client describing an activity that is incompatible with the substance use, for example, having a workout, and imagining the anticipated benefits.

The urge control strategy would be tested at each counselling session and refined in the light of the client's experience with it since the previous session. To encourage compliance with the programme it is useful to involve a significant other in at least the final part of the counselling session when homework is being assigned. This also gives an opportunity to address some of the relationship problems that arise when a client has an addiction. For example, it might be agreed between client and partner that the former goes into another room to calm down when consumed with anger and the latter is not to follow. The involvement of a significant other also enables the counsellor to check whether progress is actually being made and gains maintained outside the counselling sessions. For drugs users a random, at least monthly, urine sample should be taken and this should be scheduled into the programme from the outset. Without such 'hard' data any assessment of progress is likely to be questionable.

The client with an addiction often has multiple problems and strategies for any of the other disorders or problems may also have to be incorporated in the basic problem solving framework. Where there are multiple problems this will likely lengthen the duration of counselling.

Key point

Successful counselling for substance abuse requires sustaining problem orientation in the client. Stimulus control strategies help the client avoid drug triggers and engage in safe behaviours. Urge control strategies involve intense visualisation of the worst consequences of substance use as soon as craving begins.

---

26 Teach adult survivors of childhood trauma to separate 'then' from 'now'

Adult survivors of childhood physical and sexual abuse, as well as those exposed to mental cruelty in childhood, often continue to be haunted by their traumatic memories. In many ways they resemble clients with post-traumatic stress disorder (PTSD). Like the PTSD client there is a need to tackle the three symptom clusters of: re-experiencing the traumatic memory; avoidance – generally of intimacy; and irritability – which both reflects the frustration at not being able to sustain an intimate relationship and acts as a protective shield against perceived 'likely' attack. Strategies for tackling each of these symptom clusters are now described. However, just as many PTSD clients are also depressed so too are many adult survivors. There is then often a need to help the adult survivor challenge the early maladaptive interpretation of self (EMIS) as well as the early maladaptive expectations of others (EMEO).

I Re-experiencing

The source of the childhood trauma is often no longer accessible to the adult survivor so that any exposure to the perpetrator has to be largely imaginal. A useful strategy is to have the client 'sit' the perpetrator in an empty chair, conjure up a vivid image of the person and for about ten minutes a day at a set time say all the things that he or she ever wanted to say to the perpetrator. When experiencing intrusive recollections at other times the client is asked to calmly remind him- or herself that it is not time yet for 'the chair'. An alternative strategy is to have the client write a letter to the perpetrator at the set time expressing all of the hurts. Again, when memories intrude at other times the client has to postpone it until the writing time.

2 Avoidance

Many adult survivors experience difficulties with attachments. They either avoid intimacy altogether, perhaps provoking an argument over trivia when they want to be close to someone, or if they do make an attachment they often seek excessive reassurance that their relationship is not threatened. Some survivors alternate between these two extremes. At the root of this polarised behaviour there often lies an EMIS that the individual is flawed, defective or dirty and that intimacy will mean this 'true self' will be discovered.

One way of tackling this EMIS is to ask the client what words of comfort he or she would have for a child of the same age the client was at the time of the abuse. If the client has difficulty answering the counsellor can role play such a child who needs to be comforted. Once the client has elaborated how to reassure such a child the counsellor suggests that the client's negative feelings are really a product of the distortions he or she would have made at the age of traumatisation. It is therefore necessary when the client becomes agitated to begin to imagine comforting this younger self by challenging the latter's extreme and usually arbitrary interpretation. This can be done by asking the client to, for instance, hug a photograph of him- or herself at the age of abuse or let a cushion represent a child of that age. It is a major leap forward to get adult survivors to be gentle with themselves in this way; sometimes the jump is too big and an intermediate step has to be introduced such as imagining a child they know of the same age as themselves when abused being abused and comforting them. The more they actually care for this other child the more viable and powerful the exercise, thus if possible they would be asked to choose, say, a daughter. It will also be necessary for adult clients to inform their younger self that the EMEOs were formed in a particular context and that they represent an overgeneralisation. The EMEOs can be dislodged by the counsellor encouraging clients to collect current data on other people's behaviour. The counselling relationship itself can be a powerful contradiction of the EMEO and consequently should be given the same sort of status as in counselling clients with personality disorders. Indeed there is likely to be a substantial overlap between adult survivors and clients with personality disorders, and where there is this overlap counselling is likely to be long term.

3 Irritability

It is important with adult survivors to distinguish between the proximal causes of irritability and the distal causes. The proximal cause of the adult survivor's irritability is often a perceived unfairness in a particular situation, and a magnification of the significance of it. If others have habitually given in to (rewarded) these displays of irritability then they can be quite difficult to shift. One way forward is to suggest that this level of irritability may at most produce some short-term benefit but should the client have any further contact with the targets of irritability the latter will probably sabotage the client's wishes. In this way the counsellor is identifying with the long-term goals of the client but suggesting a better route forward. It is then possible to teach the client the anger control strategies described earlier for PTSD clients (Section 21).

The distal cause of the irritability is that life has been unfair to them. On the one hand they want intimacy but on the other they have found that it is dangerous. Realistically they have to learn to tolerate the discomfort of carrying some irritability and ambivalence. Over the years in a good relationship this irritability will probably diminish but in the short term it is necessary to accept and carry – but not act on – the feelings. The counsellor should advise the adult survivor to shout 'Stop!' when experiencing intense irritability and check out whether this irritability is actually about the 'now' or more about the 'then'. This can be done symbolically by asking the client to join his or her hands together when getting intensely irritable and ask 'Am I making the mistake of fusing "then" and "now" together?' Having answered the question the client can separate the hands widely apart, looking to, say, the left hand and saying 'That was then (followed by a very brief description)' and then to the right hand 'This is now (followed by a brief description)'. The conceptual fusion of 'then' and 'now' can greatly complicate life for adult survivors and has to be a major target for counselling.

> **Key point**
>
> Adult survivors of child abuse often experience PTSD-like symptoms. Intrusive imagery can be tackled by writing a letter to or imaginary role play with the perpetrator. Current avoidance behaviour can be approached by helping the client separate out what part of the reaction is of 'then' and which of 'now'. Strategies for tackling the irritability need to take into account both proximal and distal causes.

27 Teach clients who are victims of personality disordered family members how to distance themselves

The depression and anxiety of some clients is itself a product of interactions with personality disordered significant others, usually one or other parent, in childhood. Part of the struggle for many adults with anxiety and depression is extricating themselves from the ongoing pernicious influence of the personality disordered person. It seems to be the 'dramatic' (cluster B) and 'odd' (cluster A) personality disorders that have the most toxic influence and are more usually described by clients. Unfortunately, the 'dramatic' and 'odd' personality disordered person rarely has any stable sense of self-dissatisfaction which is a necessary condition for being open to the sort of remonstrations that the anxious or depressed client might make. Indeed the client has often laboured in vain for many years trying to change the noxious stimulus or reduce conflict by a total denial of his or her own needs.

The first step in helping the client is to assemble descriptions of conflicts with significant others using the personality disorder framework. For example, Sally was severely depressed and she described how her mother had insisted she travel five miles into town by public transport at night to hand in a prescription at the all-night chemist, when her local chemist would be open the next day and the prescription was for a further supply of a medication that her mother would not run out of for some days. The client as always reluctantly complied because of 'The scenes she creates if she does not get her own way'. Sally was particularly incensed that many of her neighbours thought her mother 'a wonderful person', and went on to comment further that any real friendships her mother had soon dissipated and the 'friend' was cast into exile and derided. The counsellor concluded that this description sounded sufficiently like Histrionic Personality Disorder (the essential feature of which is pervasive and excessive emotionality and attention seeking behaviour) to warrant further attention. At the next counselling session the counsellor asked if he could check his understanding of how her mother rated against the criteria below (note this was done without mentioning Histrionic Personality Disorder or any personality disorder to the client):

1   is uncomfortable in situations in which he or she is not the centre of attention;
2   interaction with others is often characterised by inappropriate sexually seductive or provocative behaviour;
3   displays rapidly shifting and shallow expressions of emotions;
4   constantly uses physical appearance to draw attention to self;
5   has a style of speech that is excessively impressionistic and lacking in detail;
6   shows self-dramatisation, theatricality and exaggerated expression of emotion;
7   is suggestible, that is easily influenced by others or circumstances;
8   considers relationships to be more intimate than they actually are.

The counsellor asked Sally if she could furnish examples of any of the eight symptoms. In the event Sally volunteered sufficiently clear examples to justify endorsement of symptoms 1, 3, 5, 6 and 8. Indeed there were just sufficient symptoms to meet the DSM-IV diagnostic criteria for Histrionic Personality Disorder. What was important to convey to Sally was not that her mother had a Histrionic Personality Disorder – this would have been a frightening term to her, which was never used, and a somewhat dubious one given that the counsellor had never met her mother – but instead her mother was described by the counsellor as 'Having a particular personal style' such that virtually no one could get close to her and those that tried simply got 'emotionally mangled'. This information was very important for Sally because she believed her inability to get close to her mother was her own fault and that if she just tried harder she would succeed. Ultimately Sally accepted that there was 'no pleasing' her mother and that 'a mother's love' was not a necessary condition for happiness. Thereafter, Sally increasingly kept her mother at bay, visiting her less often, controlling the speed at which she acceded to her requests and thereby 'inhaling' less of the 'toxic fumes' emitted by her.

This phenomenon is not confined to parent–child relationships but can occur also with couples. In the case of couples distress, often one partner has coped by giving way to the personality disordered partner for many years until the latter eventually exceeds the tolerance threshold of the partner, for example by having an affair. At this point the non-personality disordered partner re-evaluates the whole nature of the relationship. At this juncture it can be very illuminating and reassuring for the client to go through the appropriate diagnostic criteria as above.

The essence of helping clients with a personality disordered relative is therefore to wean the former off excessive self-blame and to legitimate an appropriate degree of distancing.

Key point

Check out whether a client's distress is a response to ongoing interactions with a significant other who has a 'dramatic' or 'odd' personality disorder. Help the client not to personalise his or her difficulty in interacting with such a significant other and teach protective strategies.

V   Quality Control

28 Assess your competence as a cognitive-behavioural counsellor

A counsellor can check his or her competence by having a live observer present at a counselling session or by having the session audio- or video-taped. It is important, however, that what is observed is checked against some agreed and explicit standard. To this end Young and Beck (1980) produced a counsellors' competency checklist with depressed clients in mind, though only minor modifications of the checklist are necessary to encompass the counselling of other emotional disorders.

The checklist for depression is reproduced in full in Appendix A and the main features of it are now discussed. The checklist is in four parts: Part I: General therapeutic skills; Part II: Conceptualization, strategy and technique; Part III: Additional considerations; and Part IV: Overall ratings and comments. Each part assesses a number of competencies each of which are rated on a seven-point scale.

In Part I six competencies are assessed. The first is 'agenda' in which the observer rates the extent to which the counsellor negotiated and followed through an agenda in the session. This particular competence reflects an ability to balance structure with empathy. The second competence is 'feedback' in which the observer rates the extent to which the counsellor checks out the client's understanding and view of what they have heard or experienced in the session. The focus here is on a detailed understanding of what the client is taking from the session as opposed to assuming that the client is taking precisely that which the counsellor would wish. The third competence is 'understanding' in which the observer rates the degree to which the counsellor is able to enter the internal reality of the client. This ability includes a responsiveness to both verbal and non-verbal communications as well as being able to put aside preconceptions. The fourth competence 'interpersonal effectiveness' requires the observer to rate the extent to which the counsellor displays optimal levels of warmth, concern, confidence, genuineness and professionalism. The fifth competence 'collaboration' requires a rating of whether the counsellor could join with the client on a problem that both considered important. The final competence assessed in Part I is 'pacing and efficient use of time' in which the observer rates the degree to which the counsellor deploys time on those things which are the most important.

Part II of the Cognitive Therapy Scale relates to competencies specific to cognitive-behavioural counselling. The first such competence is 'guided discovery' in which the counsellor is rated for the ability to help the client examine evidence, consider alternatives, weigh advantages and disadvantages rather than debate, persuade or lecture. The client is put in the role of being a scientist about his or her own experience while the counsellor is simply a collaborator. The second competence assesses whether the counsellor has made a working model of the client's difficulties and involves 'focusing on key cognitions and behaviours' as opposed to randomly targeting negative thoughts. The third competence, 'strategy for change', involves selection of the most appropriate cognitive-behavioural techniques and whether the overall strategy for change seemed promising. In the fourth competence, 'application of cognitive-behavioural techniques', the counsellor is rated on how skilfully the chosen technique is applied. The fifth and final competence in Part II relates to 'homework', both reviewing homework from previous sessions and setting homework that incorporated material learnt in the session. In this connection the authors have found it useful to summarise the counselling session in the form of a written homework for the client, compliance with which is reviewed at the next session.

Part III of the Cognitive Therapy Scale addresses two additional considerations. The first is whether any special problems arose in the session such as non-compliance with homework and how well these difficulties were handled. Clients with coexisting personality disorders are particularly likely to present additional problems. The second item asks whether there were any unusual factors present at the session that justified departure from the standard approach. For example if the client had just had a close relative die, this would probably take precedence over the anticipated session foci.

In Part IV the counsellor is given an overall rating of how well he or she conducted the session and whether the counsellor would be selected for an outcome study. The final rating is of the degree of difficulty the particular client posed. Again one would anticipate that clients with personality disorders or multiple crises would be more challenging for any counsellor and this must be taken into account when rating the therapist. At the end of the Cognitive Therapy Scale the rater is asked to make suggestions for improvement.

Key point

The effective cognitive-behavioural counsellor requires not just the empathy, warmth and genuineness of the traditional counsellor but also high levels of technical skill as comparative outcome studies suggest the former are necessary, but not sufficient, for long-term success in treatment (e.g. Covi et al., 1974; Klerman et al., 1974).

---

29 Look to outcome studies in order to have realistic expectations of what can be achieved with a client

The results of outcome studies on the efficacy of cognitive-behavioural counselling are impressive indeed. An intention-to-treat meta-analysis by the Depression Guideline Panel (1993) of 29 randomised controlled trials suggested that in acute treatment the efficacy of cognitive therapy was a 47 per cent reduction in start scores, of interpersonal therapy 52 per cent (based on one trial only) and of brief dynamic psychotherapy 35 per cent. However, there was a trend for cognitive therapy to have a lower relapse rate than interpersonal therapy (Shea et al., 1992); indeed cognitive-behavioural counselling appears to have approximately half the relapse rate of antidepressant medication. The particular strength of the cognitive-behavioural approach seems to be that because it teaches coping skills it can help prevent relapse (Morrison et al., 1995). Though depression is the most researched of the various disorders there is evidence of the efficacy of CBC from controlled trials with para-suicidal clients (Salkovskis et al., 1990), generalised anxiety disorder (Butler et al., 1987), panic disorder (Ost, 1987), and bulimia nervosa (Treasure et al., 1994).

Cognitive-behavioural counselling is invariably superior to a waiting-list treatment as usual condition and group treatment is often as efficacious as individual treatment (Scott and Stradling, 1990). Other studies (for example, Teasdale et al., 1984) have shown that early response to cognitive therapy is predictive of subsequent outcome. The standard cognitive-behavioural approaches used have been described in Scott (1989) and Trower et al. (1988). However, the success of CBC in controlled trials simply means that on average clients undergoing CBC do better or as well as other treatment modalities. This conceals the fact that there are very varying responses to CBC. To take cognitive-behavioural marital therapy as an example, it has been demonstrated that this form of counselling is superior to a waiting-list control condition (O'Leary and Beech, 1990) but that only 35–40 per cent of treated couples in the published outcome studies had post-therapy marital adjustment scores in the non-distressed range (Jacobsen et al., 1987).

The position with clients with 'odd' (cluster A) or 'dramatic' (cluster B) personality disorders is even more problematic. While Linehan et al. (1991) have managed to provide a treatment for borderline personality disordered women that was effective in that it significantly reduced para-suicidal behaviours, it did not reduce levels of depression compared with treatment as usual in the community. Linehan et al.'s counselling programme involved weekly individual and group therapy sessions for a year, something which is likely to be beyond the resources of the British NHS on a routine basis. Eighty-three per cent of these very disturbed clients remained in the counselling programme for the year. Given the success of the Salkovskis et al. (1990) brief problem solving therapy with para-suicidal clients it is possible that this might be as effective as the labour intense Linehan programme with borderline personality disordered clients. Beck et al. (1990) have suggested that the way forward with antisocial personality disordered clients is to identify with their life goals but to suggest more efficient and socially acceptable means of achieving these goals. This approach has an intuitive validity but it is still extremely difficult to engage these clients in treatment and where they have been engaged it is usually because of some legal mandate. Clearly CBC cannot rest on its laurels and is in need of continual development and refinement.

Counsellors can become dismayed that they do not routinely achieve the same results with their clients as reported in outcome studies, but it has to be remembered that many of the studies typically involve middle-class clients and that the exclusion criteria employed in research studies usually remove any patients with coexisting addictive or physical conditions. For example the client who is referred for depression who admits that his or her occasional bouts of drunkenness causes some problems would likely be excluded from a controlled trial on depression and yet would typically be treated in practice with a standard programme for depression. Similarly many of the very successful cognitive-behavioural treatments for panic disorder have often confined themselves to populations with either mild or mild-to-moderate agoraphobic avoidance, yet a practitioner may be attempting to use the same strategies with a client with a severe condition.

Expectations have also to be revised downwards because of social factors associated with the population under study. For example, Organista et al. (1994) report a 58 per cent drop-out rate in a sample of depressed patients treated using cognitive-behaviour therapy. Their US sample was low income, with two-thirds non-white, and half the total sample had a serious medical condition as well as depression. This contrasts with the 5–20 per cent drop-out rates typically reported in other outcome studies. For patient completers in the Organista et al. (1994) study there were statistically significant pre- to post-treatment reductions in depression scores but not to the same extent as results generally reported in the outcome literature.

The appropriateness of strategies will also depend on the client's readiness or motivation for change. This can be seen most obviously in the field of addictive disorders. For example, it may be entirely appropriate to discuss with one problem drinker coping strategies for handling the precipitants of relapse, yet it may be premature to discuss these with another problem drinker who has been pushed, say, by the legal system into a consultation with a counsellor. The intent in discussing the issue of motivation, in the next section, is not to attach the debilitating label of 'unmotivated' to the client but to better match strategies to client need.

Key point

The efficacy of cognitive-behavioural counselling depends on the client's particular disorder or problem and any associated complications. A counsellor has to be mindful of the selection of clear-cut cases for inclusion in outcome studies in order to avoid demoralisation.

30   Monitor and sustain your client's and your own motivation

Clients arriving for counselling may have very different agendas. DeShazer (1988) characterises three types: customer, complainant and visitor. Most counsellor training is geared to meeting the needs of the customer. The customer is clear about the problem, states that help is required to resolve the problem and have taken steps in the past to solve difficulties. The complainant has a vague description of the problem and may or may not have taken steps in the past to remedy the problem. The visitor is usually being coerced into treatment. It may not be immediately apparent which category a client falls into. The elaboration likelihood model of persuasion (ELM) can be used both to assess motivational state and to enhance it (Petty and Cacioppo, 1986; Stoltenberg et al., 1989).

In the ELM model various source (in this case, counsellor), message, recipient (in this case, client) and context factors interact in a complex manner to produce attitude change. Two main routes to persuasion are suggested – the central route and the peripheral route. The central route requires more effort and more active cognitive processing on the part of the client resulting in relatively permanent attitudes that are predictive of subsequent behaviour. The peripheral route requires minimal cognitive effort, relying on cues in the situation or rather simple decision rules. Attitudes resulting from this route are relatively temporary and are not nearly as predictive of subsequent behaviour. For example, a depressed client may engage in a homework assignment to timetable into the week some potentially uplifting events because of the attractiveness or credibility of the counsellor (peripheral processing) rather than due to believing the counsellor's message that mood is related to activity (central processing). In these circumstances any positive changes in the client's behaviour are unlikely to be maintained.

Seeking feedback from the client is a necessary condition for determining whether information has been centrally or peripherally processed. Questions should be posed about outcome expectations – for example, 'How worthwhile do you think it would be to do X?' Because there is evidence that people become more committed to that which they verbalise, any sort of positive response to the outcome expectation question should be followed by a request for further elaboration – for example, 'What makes you think that it might be worthwhile?' To somewhat understate the client's case for a positive behaviour change often produces a further more fervent elaboration of the case for performing the action – for example, 'So you think you might feel a little better if you did X successfully?' It is important, however, to check out not only a client's outcome expectations but also his or her belief in the ability to perform the task, that is, the client's self-efficacy, as this is also predictive of subsequent behaviour. Deficits in self-efficacy may be remedied by first reassessing the person's track record on performing the behaviour and using this as the most reliable baseline for subsequent behaviour as opposed to using the client's current emotional state as the indicator. If the evidence is that the client has always been deficient in the particular behaviour then it will be necessary to teach a new coping skill and modify any attitudes that might block the exhibition of the skill.

While it is important that the counsellor produces high quality arguments, that is, ones that produce more favourable than unfavourable thoughts in the client, the arguments have in addition to be judged as personally consequential by the client. The case of Jane illustrates this point.

Jane was referred by her general practitioner for treatment of a severe depression. The counsellor began her on activity scheduling and in sessions 3–6 moved on to modifying her low self-esteem by contrasting her low opinion of herself with the way in which she was obviously valued by her many friends and her family. At reassessment after the sixth session the counsellor was dismayed to find that her depression score had not decreased and that on a client satisfaction questionnaire she indicated that few of her needs were being met. The counsellor had neglected to take into account important context factors, which in this case were: (1) Jane was aged 59 and working class, her subculture meant that she was deferential to authority figures such as therapists and would not dream of challenging them even if she thought they were wrong; (2) she was living in a house that was very damp which she could neither repair nor move from; and (3) she had diabetes which had already resulted in the loss of one eye. Thus though the counsellor had used high quality arguments with Jane with which she appeared to agree, in the context they lacked sufficient personal relevance. In the event the counsellor remedied the situation by making with the client a pie chart of her depression which she found amusing as she was overweight and ate to comfort herself and having her decide what size 'slices' housing, physical health, negative view of self and so on, made up the pie. The counsellor was then able to make it clear that some progress could be made by 'nibbling away' at some slices but it was going to be much harder to 'get our teeth into' some other slices. In this way both client and counsellor developed more realistic expectations.

Key point

Check that you and the client have an agreed agenda about what is to be tackled and that the client is centrally processing your message. Guard against peripheral processing in which the client uses some rule of thumb to bypass careful weighing of the arguments.

References

Alden, L. (1989) 'Short-term structured treatment for avoidant personality disorder', *Journal of Consulting and Clinical Psychology*, 57: 756–64.

American Psychiatric Association (1987) *Diagnostic and Statistical Manual of Mental Disorders*, 3rd edn (revised). Washington, DC: American Psychiatric Association.

American Psychiatric Association (1994) *Diagnostic and Statistical Manual of Mental Disorders*, 4th edn. Washington, DC: American Psychiatric Association.

Azrin, N.H., McMahon, P.T., Donohue, B., Besalel, V.A., Lapinski, K.J., Kogan, E.S., Acierno, R.E. and Galloway, E. (1994) 'Behaviour therapy for drug abuse: a controlled outcome study', *Behaviour Research and Therapy*, 38: 857–66.

Beck, A.T., Epstein, N., Brown, G. and Steer, R.A. (1988) 'An inventory for measuring clinical anxiety: psychometric properties', *Journal of Consulting and Clinical Psychology*, 56: 893–7.

Beck, A.T., Freeman, A. and Associates (1990) *Cognitive Therapy of Personality Disorders*. New York: Guilford Press.

Beck, A.T., Rush, A.J., Shaw, B.F. and Emery, G. (1979) *Cognitive Therapy of Depression*. New York: Guilford Press.

Beck, A.T., Ward, C.H., Mendelson, M., Mock, J. and Erbaugh, J. (1961) 'An inventory for measuring depression', *Archives of General Psychiatry*, 4: 561–71.

Bedrosian, R.C. and Bozicas, G.D. (1994) *Treating Family of Origin Problems: A Cognitive Approach*. New York: Guilford Press.

Butler, G., Cullington, A., Hibbert, G., Klimes, I. and Gelder, N. (1987) 'Anxiety management and persistent generalised anxiety', *British Journal of Psychiatry*, 151: 535–42.

Clark, D.M. (1994) 'A cognitive approach to social phobia', paper presented at the British Association for Behavioural and Cognitive Psychotherapies Annual Conference, University of Lancaster, 13–15 July.

Clark, D.M. and Ehlers, A. (1993) 'An overview of the cognitive theory and treatment of panic disorder', *Applied and Preventive Psychology*, 2: 131–9.

Covi, L., Lipman, R.S., Derogatis, L.R., Smith, J.E. and Pattison, J.H. (1974) 'Drugs and psychotherapy in neurotic depression', *American Journal of Psychiatry*, 131: 191–8.

Craske, M. and Barlow, D.H. (1993) 'Panic disorder and agoraphobia', in D.H. Barlow (ed.), *Clinical Handbook of Psychological Disorders*, 2nd edn. New York: Guilford Press.

Depression Guideline Panel (1993) *Depression in Primary Care: Treatment of Major Depression*. Washington: US Department of Health and Human Services.

DeShazer, S. (1988) *Clues: Investigating Solutions in Brief Therapy*. New York: W.W. Norton.

Dobson, K.S. (1988) *Handbook of Cognitive-Behavioral Therapies*. New York: Guilford Press.

Dreesen, L., Arntz, A., Luttels, C. and Sallaerts, S. (1994) 'Personality disorders do not influence the results of cognitive-behavior therapies for anxiety disorders', *Comprehensive Psychiatry*, 35: 265–74.

Ekselius, L., Lindstrom, E., von Knorring, L., Bodlund, O. and Kullgren, G. (1993) 'Personality disorders in DSM III R: categorical or dimensional?', *Acta Psychiatrica Scandinavia*, 88: 183–7.

Ellis, A. (1962) *Reason and Emotion in Psychotherapy*. New York: Lyle Stuart.

Flemming, B. and Pretzer, J.L. (1990) 'Cognitive behavioral approaches to personality disorders', in M. Hersen, R.M. Eisler and P.M.Miller (eds), *Progress in Behavior Modification*. Newbury Park: Sage.

Forgus, R. and Shulman, B. (1979) *Personality: A Cognitive View*. Englewood Cliffs, NJ: Prentice-Hall.

Hammarberg, M. (1992) 'PENN inventory for post-traumatic stress disorder: psychometric properties', *Psychological Assessment: A Journal of Consulting and Clinical Psychology*, 4: 67–76.

Hooley, J.M., Orley, J. and Teasdale, J.D. (1986) 'Levels of expressed emotion and relapse in depressed patients', *British Journal of Psychiatry*, 148: 642–7.

Horowitz, M.J., Wilner, N. and Alvarez, W. (1979) 'Impact of event scale: a measure of subjective distress', *Psychosomatic Medicine*, 41: 209–18.

Jacobsen, N.S., Schmaling, K.B. and Holtzworth-Munroe, A. (1987) 'Component analysis of behavioral marital therapy: two year follow-up and prediction of relapse', *Journal of Marital and Family Therapy*, 13: 187–95.

Klerman, G.L., Dimascio, A., Weissman, M.M., Prusoff, B.A. and Paykel, E.S. (1974) 'Treatment of depression by drugs and psychotherapy', *American Journal of Psychiatry*, 131: 186–91.

Linehan, M.M., Armstrong, H.E., Suarez, A., Allman, D. and Heard, H.S. (1991) 'Cognitive-behavioural treatment of chronically parasuicidal borderline patients', *Archives of General Psychiatry*, 48: 1060–4.

Liotti, G. (1986) 'Structural cognitive therapy', in W. Dryden and W. Golden (eds), *Cognitive-Behavioural Approaches to Psychotherapy*. London: Harper & Row.

Mathews, A.M., Gelder, M.G. and Johnston, D.W. (1981) *Agoraphobia: Nature and Treatment*. New York: Guilford Press.

Meichenbaum, D. (1985) *Stress Inoculation Training*. New York: Pergamon Press.

Morrison, A.P., Scott, M.J. and Stradling, S.G. (1995) 'Dimensions of coping and life events as predictors of depression following cognitive therapy', *Clinical Psychology and Psychotherapy*, 2: 40–6.

Nezu, A.M., Nezu, C.M. and Perri, M.G. (1989) *Problem Solving Therapy for Depression*. New York: John Wiley.

Nietzel, M.T., Russell, R.L., Hemmings, K.D. and Gretter, M.L. (1987) 'Clinical significance of psychotherapy for unipolar depression: a meta-analytic approach to social comparison', *Journal of Consulting and Clinical Psychology*, 55: 156–61.

O'Leary, K.D. and Beach, S.R.H. (1990) 'Marital therapy: a viable treatment for depression and marital discord', *American Journal of Psychiatry*, 147: 183–6.

Organista, K.C., Munoz, R.F. and Gonzalez, G. (1994) 'Cognitive-behavioral therapy for depression in low-income and minority medical outpatients: description of a program and exploratory analyses', *Cognitive Therapy and Research*, 18: 241–60.

Ost, L.G. (1987) 'Applied relaxation: description of a coping technique and review of controlled studies', *Behaviour Research and Therapy*, 25: 397–410.

Petty, R.E. and Cacioppo, J.T. (1986) 'The elaboration likelihood model of persuasion', *Advances in Experimental Social Psychology*, 19: 123–205.

Prochaska, J.O. and DiClemente, C.C. (1984) *The Transtheoretical Approach: Crossing the Traditional Boundaries of Therapy*. Homewood, IL: Dow Jones-Irwin.

Rapee, R. (1991) 'Generalized anxiety disorder: a review of clinical features and theoretical concepts', *Clinical Psychology Review*, 11: 419–40.

Roemer, L., Borkovec, M., Posa, S. and Lyonfields, J. (1991) 'Generalized anxiety disorder in an analogue population: the role of past trauma', poster presented at the 25th Annual Convention of the Association for the Advancement of Behavior Therapy, New York, November.

Rollnick, S., Heather, N. and Bell, A. (1992) 'Negotiating behaviour change in medical settings: the development of brief motivational interviewing', *Journal of Mental Health*, 1: 25–37.

Salkovskis, P.M., Atha, C. and Storer, D. (1990) 'Cognitive-behavioural problem solving in the treatment of patients who repeatedly attempt suicide: a controlled trial', *British Journal of Psychiatry*, 157: 871–6.

Scott, M.J. (1989) *A Cognitive-Behavioural Approach to Clients' Problems*. London: Tavistock/Routledge.

Scott, M.J. and Stradling, S.G. (1990) 'Group cognitive therapy for depression produces clinically significant reliable change in community-based settings', *Behavioural Psychotherapy*, 18: 1–19.

Scott, M.J. and Stradling, S.G. (1992) *Counselling for Post-Traumatic Stress Disorder*. London: Sage.

Scott, M.J., Stradling, S.G. and Greenfield, T.A. (1994a) 'The effect of brief group cognitive therapy on generalised anxiety disorder and panic disorder patients and the significance of a personality disorder diagnosis', paper presented to Symposium on 'Developments in the Conceptualisation and Treatment of Anxiety' (organisers M.J. Scott and S.G. Stradling), British Association for Behavioural and Cognitive Psychotherapies Annual Conference, University of Lancaster, 13–15 July.

Scott, M.J., Stradling, S.G. and Greenfield, T.A. (1994b) 'The effect of brief group cognitive therapy on depressed patients and the significance of a personality disorder diagnosis', paper presented at British Association for Behavioural and Cognitive Psychotherapies Annual Conference, University of Lancaster, 13–15 July.

Shea, M.T., Elkin, I., Imber, S.D., Sotsky, S.M., Watkins, J.T., Collins, J.F., Pilkonis, P.A., Beckham, E., Glass, D.R., Dolan, R.T. and Parloff, M.B. (1992) 'Course of depressive symptoms over follow-up: findings from the National Institute of Mental Health treatment of depression collaborative research program', *Archives of General Psychiatry*, 49: 782–7.

Snaith, R.P. and Zigmond, A.S. (1983) 'The hospital anxiety and depression scale', *Acta Psychiatrica Scandinavia*, 67: 361–70.

Spitzer, R.L., Williams, J.B.W., Gibbon, M. and First, M. (1990) *Structured Clinical Interview for the DSM III R Personality Disorders* (SCID 2, version 1.0). Washington, DC: American Psychiatric Association.

Stoltenberg, C.D., Leach, M.M. and Bratt, A. (1989) 'The elaboration likelihood model of persuasion and psychotherapeutic persuasion', *Journal of Cognitive Psychotherapy*, 3: 181–200.

Teasdale, J.D., Fennell, M.J.V., Hibbert, G.A. and Amies, P.L. (1984) 'Cognitive therapy for major depressive disorder in primary care', *British Journal of Psychiatry*, 144: 400–6.

Treasure, J., Schmidt, U., Troop, N., Tiller, J., Todd, G., Keilen, M. and Dodge, E. (1994) 'First step in managing bulimia nervosa: controlled trial of a therapeutic manual', *British Medical Journal*, 308: 686–9.

Trower, P., Casey, A. and Dryden, W. (1988) *Cognitive-Behavioural Counselling in Action*. London: Sage.

Wells, A. (1994) 'A multi-dimensional measure of worry: development and preliminary validation of the anxious thoughts inventory', *Anxiety, Stress and Coping*. 6: 289–99.

Wessler, R. (1993) 'Cognitive psychotherapy approaches to personality disorders', *Psicologia Conductual*, 1: 35–48.

Williams, S.J. and Mark. G. (1992) *The Psychological Treatment of Depression*, 2nd edn. London: Routledge.

Young, J.E. (1990) *Cognitive Therapy for Personality Disorders: A Schema-Focused Approach*. Sarasota: Professional Resource Exchange.

Young, J.E. (1994) *Cognitive Therapy for Personality Disorders: A Schema-Focused Approach*, revised edn. Sarasota: Professional Resource Exchange.

Young, J.E. and Beck, A.T. (1980) *Cognitive Therapy Scale Rating Manual*. Philadelphia: Centre for Cognitive Therapy, University of Pennsylvania.

Zettle, R.D., Haflich, J.L. and Reynolds, R.A. (1992) 'Responsivity to cognitive therapy as a function of treatment format and client personality dimensions', *Journal of Clinical Psychology*, 48: 787–97.

Appendix A
Beck's Cognitive Therapy Scale*

Directions:

For each item, assess the therapist on a scale from 0 to 6 and record the rate on the line next to the item number. Descriptions are provided for even-number scale points. *If you believe the therapist falls between two of the descriptions select the intervening odd number (1,3,5).* For example, if the therapist sets very good agenda but did not establish priorities, assign a rating of 5 rather than 4 or 6.

If the descriptions for a given item occasionally do not seem to apply to the session you are rating, feel free to disregard them and use the more general scale below:

0	1	2	3	4	5	6
Poor	Barely Adequate	Mediocre	Satisfactory	Good	Very good	Excellent

Please do not leave any item blank. For all items, focus on the skill of the therapist, taking into account how difficult the patient seems to be.

Part I. GENERAL THERAPEUTIC SKILLS

1. AGENDA

0 Therapist did not set agenda.

2 Therapist set agenda that was vague or incomplete.

4 Therapist worked with patient to set a mutually satisfactory agenda that includes specific target problems (e.g. anxiety at work, dissatisfaction with marriage).

6 Therapist worked with patient to set an appropriate agenda with target problems, suitable for the available time. Established priorities and then followed the agenda.

Reproduced with permission from J.E. Young and A.T. Beck (1980) *Cognitive Therapy Scale Rating Manual.*

2.   FEEDBACK

0   Therapist did not ask for feedback to determine patient's understanding of, or response to, the session.

2   Therapist elicited some feedback from the patient, but did not ask enough questions to be sure the patient understood the therapist's line of reasoning during the session *or* to ascertain whether the patient was satisfied with the session.

4   Therapist asked enough questions to be sure that the patient understood the therapist's line of reasoning throughout the session and to determine the patient's reactions to the session. The therapist adjusted his/her behavior in response to the feedback, when appropriate.

6   Therapist was especially adept at eliciting and responding to verbal and non-verbal feedback throughout the session (e.g. elicited reactions to session, regularly checked for understanding, helped summarize main points at end of session).

3.   UNDERSTANDING

0   Therapist repeatedly failed to understand what the patient explicitly said and thus consistently missed the point. Poor empathic skills.

2   Therapist was usually able to reflect or rephrase what the patient explicitly said, but repeatedly failed to respond to more subtle communication. Limited ability to listen and empathize.

4   Therapist generally seemed to grasp the patient's 'internal reality' as reflected by both what the patient explicitly said and what the patient communicated in more subtle ways. Good ability to listen and empathize.

6   Therapist seemed to understand the patient's 'internal reality' thoroughly and was adept at communicating this understanding through appropriate verbal and non-verbal responses to the patient (e.g. the tone of the therapist's response conveyed a sympathetic understanding of the patient's 'message'). Excellent listening and empathic skills.

4.   INTERPERSONAL EFFECTIVENESS

0   Therapist had poor interpersonal skills. Seemed hostile, demeaning, or in some other way destructive to the patient.

2   Therapist did not seem destructive, but had significant interpersonal problems. At times, therapist appeared unnecessarily impatient, aloof, insincere *or* had difficulty conveying confidence and competence.

4   Therapist displayed a *satisfactory* degree of warmth, concern, confidence, genuineness and professionalism. No significant interpersonal problems.

6   Therapist displayed *optimal* levels of warmth, concern, confidence, genuineness and professionalism, appropriate for this particular patient in this session.

5.   COLLABORATION

0   Therapist did not attempt to set up a collaboration with patient.

2   Therapist attempted to collaborate with patient, but had difficulty *either* defining a problem that the patient considered important *or* establishing rapport.

4   Therapist was able to collaborate with patient, focus on a problem that both patient and therapist considered important, and establish rapport.

6   Collaboration seemed excellent; therapist encouraged patient as much as possible to take an active role during the session (e.g. by offering choices) so they could function as a 'team'.

6.   PACING AND EFFICIENT USE OF TIME

0   Therapist made no attempt to structure therapy time. Session seemed aimless.

2   Session had some direction, but the therapist had significant problems with structuring or pacing (e.g. too little structure, inflexible about structure, too slowly paced, too rapidly paced).

4   Therapist was reasonably successful at using time efficiently. Therapist maintained appropriate control over flow of discussion and pacing.

6   Therapist used time very efficiently by tactfully limiting peripheral and unproductive discussion and by pacing the session as rapidly as was appropriate for the patient.

Part II.   CONCEPTUALIZATION, STRATEGY, AND
            TECHNIQUE

7.   GUIDED DISCOVERY

0   Therapist relied primarily on debate, persuasion, or 'lectur-
    ing'. Therapist seemed to be 'cross-examining' patient,
    putting the patient on the defensive, or forcing his/her point
    of view on the patient.

2   Therapist relied too heavily on persuasion and debate, rather
    than guided discovery. However, therapist's style was
    supportive enough that patient did not seem to feel attacked
    or defensive.

4   Therapist, for the most part, helped patient see new perspec-
    tives through guided discovery (e.g. examining evidence,
    considering alternatives, weighing advantages and disadvan-
    tages) rather than through debate. Used questioning appro-
    priately.

6   Therapist was especially adept at using guided discovery
    during the session to explore problems and help patient draw
    his/her own conclusions. Achieved an excellent balance
    between skilful questioning and other modes of intervention.

8.   FOCUSING ON KEY COGNITIONS OR BEHAVIORS

0   Therapist did not attempt to elicit specific thoughts, assump-
    tions, images, meanings, or behaviors.

2   Therapist used appropriate techniques to elicit cognitions or
    behaviors; however, therapist had difficulty finding a focus *or*
    focused on cognition/behaviors that were irrelevant to the
    patient's key problems.

4   Therapist focused on specific cognitions or behaviors relevant
    to the target problem. However, therapist could have focused
    on more central cognitions or behavior that offered greater
    promise for progress.

6   Therapist very skilfully focused on key thoughts, assump-
    tions, behaviors, etc. that were most relevant to the problem
    area and offered promise for progress.

9. STRATEGY FOR CHANGE (Note: For this item, focus on the quality of the therapist's strategy for change, not on how effectively the strategy was implemented or whether change actually occurred.)

0   Therapist did not select cognitive-behavioral techniques.

2   Therapist selected cognitive-behavioral techniques; however, either the overall strategy for bringing about change seemed vague *or* did not seem promising in helping the patient.

4   Therapist seemed to have a generally coherent strategy for change that showed reasonable promise and incorporated cognitive-behavioral techniques.

6   Therapist followed a consistent strategy for change that seemed very promising and incorporated the most appropriate cognitive-behavioral techniques.

10. APPLICATION OF COGNITIVE-BEHAVIORAL TECHNI-QUES (Note: for this item, focus on how skilfully the techniques were applied, not on how appropriate they were for the target problem or whether change actually occurred.)

0   Therapist did not apply any cognitive-behavioral techniques.

2   Therapist used cognitive-behavioral techniques, but there were *significant flaws* in the way they were applied.

4   Therapist applied cognitive-behavioral techniques *with moderate skill.*

6   Therapist *very skilfully* and resourcefully employed cognitive-behavioural techniques.

11. HOMEWORK

0   Therapist did not attempt to incorporate homework relevant to cognitive therapy.

2   Therapist had significant difficulties incorporating homework (e.g. did not review previous homework, did not explain homework in sufficient detail, assigned inappropriate home-work).

4   Therapist reviewed previous homework and assigned 'standard' cognitive therapy homework generally relevant to

issues dealt with in session. Homework was explained in sufficient detail.

6   Therapist reviewed previous homework and carefully assigned homework drawn from cognitive therapy for the coming week. Assignment seemed 'custom tailored' to help patient incorporate new perspectives, test hypotheses, experiment with new behaviors discussed during session, etc.

Part III.   ADDITIONAL CONSIDERATIONS

12   (a) Did any special problems arise during the session (e.g. non-adherence to homework, interpersonal issues between therapist and patient, hopelessness about continuing therapy, relapse)?

YES   NO

(b) *If yes*:

0   Therapist could not deal adequately with special problems that arose.

2   Therapist dealt with special problems adequately, but used strategies or conceptualizations inconsistent with cognitive therapy.

4   Therapist attempted to deal with special problems using a cognitive framework and was *moderately skilful* in applying techniques.

6   Therapist was very skilful at handling special problems using cognitive therapy framework.

13.   Were there any significant unusual factors in this session that you feel justified the therapist's departure from the standard approach measured by this scale?

YES (please explain below)   NO

Part IV.   OVERALL RATINGS AND COMMENTS

14.   How would you rate the clinician overall in this session, as a cognitive therapist:

0	1	2	3	4	5	6
Poor	Barely Adequate	Mediocre	Satisfactory	Good	Very good	Excellent

15. If you were conducting an outcome study in cognitive therapy, do you think you would select this therapist to participate at this time (assuming this session is typical)?

0	1	2	3	4
Definitely Not	Probably Not	Uncertain Borderline	Probably Yes	Definitely Yes

16. How difficult did you feel this patient was to work with?

0	1	2	3	4	5	6
Not difficult, very receptive			Moderately difficult			Extremely difficult

17. COMMENTS AND SUGGESTIONS FOR THERAPIST'S IMPROVEMENT:

This scale is not intended to be used for the initial interview or final session with a patient.

For instructions on the use of this scale, see: J.E. Young and A.T. Beck, *Cognitive Therapy Scale Rating Manual* August, 1980.

* For permission to use the scale or a copy of the Rating Manual, please write: Centre for Cognitive Therapy, University of Pennsylvania, Room 602, 133 S. 36th St., Philadelphia, PA 19104, USA.

Index